Learning with Mobile and Handheld Technologies

GW00992219

As technology evolves we are ever more reliant on .... devices, yet what do we know about their impact on learning? While there is a lot of interest in mobile technology, many schools still aren't sure how to best use it for learning and teaching.

Learning with Mobile and Handheld Technologies explores this landscape and offers examples of how these technologies have been used for learning, how the problems that have arisen are being addressed, and offers ideas for the future. This invaluable book gives a voice to teachers and educators using mobiles and technology-enhanced learning in and out of schools, for regular school work and for innovative projects through exciting partnerships like Apps for Good.

Learning with Mobile and Handheld Technologies shows the changes that are taking place within schools as a direct result of these emerging technologies, and contains case studies with accounts of best practice in a variety of settings including primary, secondary, and special schools, and learning beyond their boundaries. The book also explores themes of pedagogy, communication and affordances, collaborative learning, individual creativity and expression, self-directed and informal learning.

The learning potential of handheld and mobile devices has excited teachers and educators, but until now there has been no structured, systematic overview available along with reflections on how this technology is changing educational practice. This book brings these together to provide a clearer picture of what is currently a fragmented area, and offers expert views of how we can understand these, and where it may take us next.

John Galloway is an adviser, writer and consultant, specialising in ICT for SEN and inclusion. He has worked with several local authorities and just about every sort of school. He has been involved in several projects that have used handheld devices with learners, and provides training for teachers and other staff at every level from beginner to post-graduate. He is the author of four David Fulton titles.

Merlin John is a journalist who has written extensively about this field. Previously editor of The Times Educational Supplement's Online magazine, he now manages his own website, www.agent4change.net, a source of information for using technology for learning.

Maureen McTaggart previously worked for TSL Education Limited, publisher of The Times Educational Supplement and the Times Higher Education Supplement. She is now a freelance writer, mainly in the field of ICT in education, and part-time in the publishing and communications departments at the School of Advanced Study, University of London.

Learning with Mobile and Handheld Technologies

John Galloway, Merlin John and Maureen McTaggart

Routledge
Taylor & Francis Group

LONDON AND NEW YORK

First published 2015
by Routledge
2 Park Square, Milton Park, Abingdon, Oxon OX14 4RN

and by Routledge
711 Third Avenue, New York, NY 10017

Routledge is an imprint of the Taylor & Francis Group, an informa business

British Library Cataloguing in Publication Data
A catalogue record for this book is available from the British Library

Library of Congress Cataloging in Publication Data
Galloway, John (Educational technology consultant)
Learning with mobile and handheld technologies/John Galloway,
Merlin John, and Maureen McTaggart.
pages cm
1. Mobile communication systems in education. 2. Information technology.
3. Pocket computers. I. John, Merlin. II. McTaggart, Maureen. III. Title.
LB1044.84.G35 2015
371.33–dc23
2014021195

ISBN: 978-0-415-84249-5 (hbk)
ISBN: 978-0-415-84250-1 (pbk)
ISBN: 978-1-315-74183-3 (ebk)

Typeset in Bembo
by Swales & Willis Ltd, Exeter, Devon, UK

Contents

Preface

It can't have escaped anyone's attention that the mobile technology revolution is affecting education. It has been a long time coming, but finally, highly portable devices are popping up in classrooms everywhere, offering new possibilities for teaching and learning and creating a bit of a buzz. While some schools have been quick to exploit it, others are slow to change.

Mobile technology, and the wireless networks on which it depends, is now sufficiently robust, easy to use and affordable for schools to commit to its adoption. Terms like 1:1 computing, BYOD (bring your own device) and BYOT (bring your own technology) are signalling the cusp that schools are moving into. Even with a change of government, from one that pumped millions of pounds of ring-fenced money into technology in schools to one that appears completely unmoved by the possibilities on offer, the bandwagon continues to roll. The machines that are available today can truly transform what happens in, and out, of classrooms.

Carl Faulkner, award-winning headteacher at Normanby Primary School, Middlesbrough, demonstrates this in this reflection on school use of digital video:

> When we first started using video I would carry the video camera and a colleague would walk behind me carrying the battery. It might take us a month to edit the footage. Now my learners can shoot a video on their iPod Touches, edit it on the fly, and if they don't like it they can reshoot.

The challenge for schools is to keep the learning in the driving seat so they can unlock the full benefit of the changes that mobile technology can bring. This book aims to help them.

It takes a journalistic rather than an academic approach – telling stories and canvassing opinions. Readers who are looking for statistical 'evidence' of learning gains, sadly also frequently requested by people who only seek to obstruct and delay, should look elsewhere. Here the proof comes from the voices of committed professionals, investing more than money to change their practice and enhancing learning for their pupils across all phases of education in every type of school.

Educators are constantly asked to make a case for why technology should be used for learning and teaching, in and out of school. Perhaps the time has come to ask instead, where it isn't being put to good use, why not? Don't we want to use the most innovative, creative, exciting technologies, to support and drive the most engaging, effective, enjoyable learning?

This book aims to tell the story of changes in learning and teaching in the UK, supported and accelerated by mobile technology that can better serve learners and connect them to a life of learning. It hasn't aimed to be fully comprehensive and inclusive, covering every device, situation and subject, but is a reasonable attempt by three people with a desire to share stories from classrooms across the country to throw some light on what is happening, and help those who want to join this quiet revolution along their way.

We talked to educators, academics, developers and consultants across the spectrum, here and abroad, about schools that are leading the way and who want to share their excitement about what they are discovering with the wider education community.

Acknowledgements

This book would not have been possible without the generosity of teachers and educators in the UK and beyond. The fundamental purpose of teaching and learning is to share knowledge, which the schools, experts, developers and other professionals who have helped us have done with unstinting openness and support for our project. It is a heart-warming demonstration that, at its heart, education is a collaborative, cooperative endeavour, driven by a belief in our shared responsibility to this broad and committed community, and to our children and young people.

In particular we would like to thank the staff and learners in the schools that opened their doors to us for the case studies: the Flitch Green Academy in Essex; Normanby Primary School in Middlesbrough; Oakdale Junior School in Redbridge, London; Essa Academy, Bolton; Cramlington Learning Village, Northumberland; Woodlawn School, Whitley Bay; and Frank Wise School, Banbury.

Many other people in schools and across all aspects of education freely contributed their ideas and expertise. As did journalist Steve Swain with his heroic proof-reading work.

Several people helped us to understand the role of tablets to support inclusion, particularly for children and young people with special educational needs. They include Sally Paveley and Stephen Drewitt of the Bridge School, Islington; Ben Annett of Riverside School, Haringey; Martin Littler and Roger Bates of Inclusive Technology and HelpKidzLearn Inc; Richard Hirstwood of Hirstwood Training; and Anna Reeves, of ACE Centre North.

We also had many thoughtful and reflective responses to our questions from our panel of experts and academics: Dewi Lloyd, independent consultant; Carol Allen, school improvement adviser for ICT and inclusion in North Tyneside; Dan Buckley, deputy headteacher of Saltash.net Community College; Abdul Chohan, director at Essa Academy; Dave Whyley, independent consultant; Vanessa Pittard at the Department for Education; Elizabeth Hartnell-Young, director of the Australian Council for Educational Research; Jocelyn Wishart, senior lecturer in education at the Graduate School of Education, University of Bristol; Professor Stephen Heppell, who is based at Bournemouth University as chair in new media environments at the Centre for Excellence in Media Practice at Bournemouth, visiting professor in Madrid, Emeritus Professor at Anglia Ruskin; Dr Christina Preston, founder of Mirandanet and professor of Educational Innovation at the University of Bedfordshire; Mal Lee, education consultant; Professor Miguel Nussbaum of The Catholic University of Chile; Andrew Rhodes of the International School, Stavanger, Norway; and Professor Don Passey of Lancaster University.

Finally, we need to thank our families for giving us the space to get on and write when we needed it, and helping to smooth the bumps along the way.

John Galloway, Merlin John and Maureen McTaggart

The context

Introduction

> Mobile learning is a term used to define the type of learning that takes place when the learner has some kind of mobile computer, making use of its connectivity, location awareness, content and applications to learn at a time and place of the learner's choosing.
>
> (Wolverhampton's Learning2Go)

In other words, 'Having available the full range of resources and capability that ICT offers in the best classroom – at all times and in all places' (Dave Whyley, education consultant who led the Learning2Go project in Wolverhampton).

The headlines speak for themselves: 'Every school child in Los Angeles to get an iPad' (*Daily Mail*);[1] 'Malaysia adopts Google Apps, Chromebooks for education' (Znet.com);[2] 'Kent school gives an iPad to each of its 1,400 pupils' (*Metro*).[3]

Mobile technology for learning has become, as widely and long predicted, a big story worldwide. But what is the reality behind the headlines? Where is the learning and what do teachers, school leaders, administrators, learners and their families need to know to best take advantage of the potential of mobile technologies for learning?

Despite all that has been learned in schools about putting the learning first and then attending to the technology, it seems there is no shortage of decisions that reflect the opposite when it comes to digital tablets, and Apple's iPad in particular, which was first to market and took the dominant share. Sobering reading for anyone wanting to avoid intoxication by the potential of 1:1 schemes is 'A second look at iPads in Los Angeles', a blog post by US academic Larry Cuban, an analysis of how 'The rollout of iPads in Los Angeles Unified School District (LAUSD) is becoming a classic case study of what not to do when implementing any innovation whether it is high-tech or low-tech.'[4]

Of course schools have always been interested in new and mobile technologies, but the days of technology being designed and produced specifically for them are, for the most part, gone. Consumerisation of technology is now the dominant trend.

When technology is easy to use schools can be very quick adopters. Digital cameras were an early success, as were the Flip video cameras which also helped accelerate the uptake of reflective practice, a trend that is still growing. And the ease of use that touch technology brought to mobile devices is already opening opportunities for those working in special needs and inclusion (see Chapter 2).

Once upon a time in the UK, schools conducted pilot projects with mobile technology. They were usually set up with commercial partners and technical support, and some were partnered with university researchers looking for learning gains. The area of work even had its own annual conference, Handheld Learning, created by education entrepreneur Graham Brown-Martin, which blossomed into the excellent Learning Without Frontiers before its demise in 2013.[5]

There were also research reports. One early report, produced by a team at the University of Bristol and published by the now-defunct Government ICT agency Becta in 2007, was broadly positive. While it warned that implementing a project using personal digital assistants (PDAs) was 'logistically challenging and requires careful planning and commitment from all partners', with this in place, said the report, 'promising innovative practice is likely to ensue'.[6]

Ironically, their observations chime with those of Larry Cuban in his post about the LA iPads fiasco. 'Teachers need to play an integral role', the report warned. 'Where there is a good match to needs, teachers are more likely to make use of the devices.'

With the benefit of hindsight, it's clear that the technology back in the 1990s still wasn't quite ready for anytime, anywhere use. However, the admirable optimism of educators and the enthusiasm of learners, coupled with the promise of new advances in technology, certainly fuelled impressive pilots. And the research into these was mainly positive, despite the identification of administrative issues, like managing distribution and charging, as key obstacles.

One of the first UK successes was the Docklands Learning Acceleration Project in East London, run by the National Literacy Association with partners in the mid-1990s. Around 600 7-year-olds, across some 15 schools, were issued with Acorn Pocket Book handheld computers (rebadged Psion clamshell devices). No technical issues were reported and only one was lost. Improvements were recorded in children's literacy.

The organisers were clear about the role of the ICT. Project coordinator Ray Barker, who went on to become director of the British Educational Suppliers Association (BESA), commented: 'This is a literacy not an IT initiative. The technology is only one tool for learning and is supported by more traditional methods.'[7]

Where pedagogy took the lead there were other early successes. One project in Wolverhampton's ground-breaking Learning2Go programme took primary school pupils on a field trip to Tenby in South Wales where they were able to pin their digital productions – notes, photos, videos – to maps using GPRS and newly developed software from Wild Knowledge (with on-site support from Steljes educator Dewi Lloyd). Suddenly, map making came alive for learners, and their PDAs were able to operate as the digital notebooks envisaged by pioneering staff.[8]

And over at Goldsmiths, University of London, the E-scape project demonstrated that mobile technology could be used to unlock the potential of peer evaluation to create a highly effective and accurate assessment system that impressed educators by its respect for both process and product, making it a good example of technology enabling changes in practice. Despite being overlooked by UK politicians and policy makers, what once was E-scape is now being sold to happy customers in Sweden, Israel, Ireland, the USA, Australia and Singapore as LiveAssess and ACJ.[9]

As their experience and confidence grew, UK educators specified their ideal device – an education digital assistant (EDA). This would be a digital notebook for photos, text, audio, in fact any media that could be used in support of learning. Such was the enthusiasm that a team involving Wolverhampton headteacher consultant David Whyley actually persuaded Fujitsu Siemens to manufacture one.[10]

Unfortunately, the technology still couldn't match the rapidly developing desires. But very soon it could, with the appearance of Apple's iPod Touch, even without a dedicated keyboard. This was the nearest thing to an EDA that schools had seen. 'Instant on' was a breath of fresh air for people plagued by machines that needed minutes to boot up. And an 'all-day' battery was another clincher.

Within a relatively short time projects had shifted from 'Let's try and do something interesting with this nice new device and see if there's any learning to be had,' to 'We know the kind of learning we want to do and this is the best device to support it'. And the people who turned everyone's heads by achieving this to scale – school-wide – can be found in Bolton, at Essa Academy (see Chapter 6).[11]

Through thoughtful leadership and vision, Essa Academy ranks as one of the happiest and most successful schools in the UK. 'All will succeed', its motto, is not optional. The focus is on engaging all the students in rich, effective learning, anytime and anywhere. And their first brave step, after an initial pilot and positive feedback from students, was to give everyone in the school – all learners and all staff – an iPod Touch.

Former Essa principal Showk Badat and his staff have innovated the learning at the school and the iPod was the first device to come along that best supported it. Visitors who are starstruck by the technology, and think it's an Apple story, miss the point. It's far more than that, with personalisation of learning at its heart.

The most important management message from Essa for education decision makers comes from Showk Badat, who had charts on his office walls for every department, including both their results and their costs. 'They show that the costs of getting grades A, B and C are getting smaller,' he explains. 'What appears to be a high level of cost for a particular resource, ICT, gives us a high impact on grades so it has given us better value for money.'

This school leader is very conscious of the price of success. And, for Essa, the judicious use of mobile technology to support great learning has actually lowered that price. The evidence is there to be shared. Back in 2009 Essa worked out that the cost per C+ grade was approximately £3,990. The use of ICT brought that down to £2,380 by 2010 – a saving of £1,610 (40 per cent).

Now the school has moved on. It has replaced the iPods with iPads, which were not available when the original decision was taken. Interest in Essa is at such a level that the school has timetabled public tours and, as you might expect from an innovative school, they are supported by curriculum work involving students. It might interest UK Conservative politicians, who would like state schools to be more like private schools, that one of the visits was by the English school that educated so many of the UK Coalition Government's cabinet ministers – Eton College.

Teachers and school leaders who had pioneered the use of mobile technologies now feel free to take quick steps forward as mobile devices become suitable for both school and home use. Carl Faulkner, award-winning headteacher at Normanby Primary School, Middlesbrough, demonstrates this cusp in this reflection on school use of digital video: 'When we first started using video I would carry the video camera and a colleague would walk behind me carrying the battery. It might take us a month to edit the footage. Now my learners can shoot a video on their iPod Touches, edit it on the fly, and if they don't like it they can reshoot it.'[12]

Normanby Primary School has already been carrying out its own successful 1:1 iPod Touch pilot and working on interesting new ways to integrate the exciting new technologies becoming available with teachers' own tried and tested classroom favourites (see Chapter 4). While the school's vision for learning guides its developments there is also a healthy streak of pragmatism that ensures sensible use of resources.

That's also very much the attitude at Cramlington Learning Village in Northumberland, 'Where the Art of Teaching meets the Science of Learning', according to its school motto. A state secondary school in the north-east of England, it has been at the thoughtful edge of learning and technology for a number of years, also working with developers to ensure that its teachers and learners have access to technology that supports its highly developed policies for learning and teaching (see Chapter 7).[13]

Never one to follow the crowd, Cramlington considered iPads for its 1:1 plans but opted instead for 7-inch Android devices from Samsung. Interestingly, Cramlington recognises the rapid development in technologies and does not feel itself wedded to any particular hardware platform – it does not consider itself 'an Android school' and is open to other developments, like Windows tablets.

Cramlington can take this position because it has carefully built up an impressive ICT infrastructure of virtual learning environment and curriculum content that can work with a range of hardware. It's an important point for other schools looking to adopt mobile devices for staff and students, and representatives of the school were on hand at the Tablets for Schools conference in London in December 2013 to help demonstrate the diversity and choice available.[14]

That's also important because a technology sea change is taking place in UK schools as the move to mobile devices gathers pace. And as the clamour surrounding mobile technology increases, there has been no central, independent source of objective research and advice for schools since the incoming Coalition Government closed down the national ICT education agency Becta in 2011.[15]

In fact, the new government's lack of understanding of learning with technology took educators and schools by surprise. Questions on the issue went unanswered and it took the then education secretary Michael Gove MP more than a year to make a statement on the issue. His keynote presentation to the BETT 2012 educational technology event in London that January was a superficially reassuring commitment to the importance of technology for learning. However, the technology advisory team of civil servants that had prepared the speech had been disbanded within months.[16]

The Westminster policy on ICT for learning was clear – there was no policy. Schools should work it out for themselves. Stung by criticism by Google boss Eric Schmidt of the role of technology in the English national curriculum, the government handed over responsibility for curriculum reform to BCS – the Chartered Institute for IT (known as the British Computer Society) and the Royal Academy of Engineering. The result was a new subject, Computing, heavily weighted towards computer science.[17]

It would be a mistake however to focus solely on policy for English schools. Wales, Northern Ireland and Scotland all have their own distinctive approaches to curriculum and technology deployment. Wales, in particular, is looking well placed for the adoption of mobile technology because its new Hwb national network for learning has been designed to work on all technology, from mobile phones and handhelds through digital tablets to desktop machines. And Scotland has already pioneered the use of off-the-shelf computer games, on mobile devices too (Nintendo DS), through the ground-breaking work of Derek Robertson at the sadly now-defunct Consolarium.

Despite the virtual disappearance of national UK leadership on technology for learning, schools might have reconsidered the place of ICT for learning but they certainly did not appear to relax their investments. Market research conducted by British Educational Suppliers Association (BESA) in 1,238 UK schools (731 primary and 507 secondary) indicates that they expect to spend record levels on their ICT in 2014–15.[18] (An earlier report estimated that the number of tablets in schools would rise to about 260,000 by the end of 2013, more than double the previous year, and that more than two-thirds of schools 'want to see research evidence to support the adoption of tablets in schools'.)

Secondaries expect the average spend to increase 11 per cent to £65,570 for hardware replacement, peripherals, software and support (a total for secondaries of £280 million). The percentage of school computers which are tablets is expected to rise from 10 to 24 per cent by the end of 2015.

According to the research, 14 per cent of these schools are interested in buying desktop computers, 19 per cent laptops and 77 per cent digital tablets. BESA research tends to be rather conservative, so these responses reflect the dramatic statistics for increased adoption of technology in the consumer markets for which they are designed. However, combine the reported desires of schools with the projected sums and it's not hard to see why an almost crusading quality has emerged in the education debate about tablets.

In 2013 the e-Learning Foundation, dedicated to 'bridging the digital divide', ran a conference devoted to 'Keep taking the tablets'.[19] The Tablets for Schools organisation, created by tablet and mobile phone supplier Carphone Warehouse as part of its corporate social responsibility programme, operates under the banner

'We believe tablets can transform education'. Quite how a technology can transform learning, rather than support and accelerate it, has not been fully explained.

Given the commercial stakes, it's important for decision makers to retain their critical faculties in the face of visible and increasing changes and disruption. In his article 'Touch and pads open door to SEN "dream device"', Martin Littler, an expert on ICT for special needs and inclusion, gives a flavour of the disruption caused by tablets:

> We hear of shares in communication aid companies going from more than $25 to less than 10 cents! We hear of special schools buying iPads in dozens. Meanwhile, most companies selling CD-based software into the SEN [special educational needs] sector are seeing their sales decimated.[20]

At a time of recession, when national leadership is weak or absent when it comes to learning with technology, decision making by schools and businesses can be fraught. While there is no right or wrong technology – only appropriate or not – a 'wrong' decision can be very damaging. Which is why there is a hunger for reliable research.

There are plenty of case studies and reports covering iPads in schools but few reflect the objectivity and editorial independence of a classic university-based research project. The only report of this kind so far since the disappearance of Becta has been the *iPad Scotland Evaluation* (2012), carried out by a team at the University of Hull. A clear and direct report, it listed the advantages that many observers have come to expect, like improved student engagement and anywhere, anytime learning, but it also highlighted an element that intrigues many otherwise cynical experts (see Chapter 12).[21]

The report found that, when teachers and learners all have access to mobile technology, there is the potential to change their relationships for learning:

> learning becomes more student centred and student friendly releasing the creativity of the student. The myriad apps that are available allow students to work independently, in groups and as part of the whole class, developing a range of knowledge and skills.

Education reformers like Michael Fullan (see *New Pedagogies for Deep Learning* by Michael Fullan and Maria Langworthy)[22] recognise the power of technology to support transformation of learning but warn that it is not the agent of change in itself. So, while it's easy to understand why visitors to Essa Academy might be enthusiastic about going out and buying tablets to transform learning in their schools, they would be missing the point. The school already had a very clear vision of the kind of learning it wanted to develop, and how the technology could make that possible.

The good news is that more research has been commissioned in the UK to measure the effect of technology on pupil attainment and support more informed technology choices. The Education Endowment Foundation and the Nominet

Trust have invested a total of £3.5 million in a range of projects that include mobile devices, texting services for parents and online curriculum resources for learners to use anywhere.[23]

Among a varied range of projects are:

- a £253,000 grant for Rosendale Primary School in south London to test the value of iPads in boosting learning skills

- a £559,000 grant to Shireland Community Academy in Sandwell, West Midlands to investigate the effectiveness of a 'flipped learning' approach – pupils are introduced to concepts online before using class time to investigate and discuss them further with teachers and peers

- a £532,000 grant to a joint team from Harvard and Bristol University to work with 34 schools to test whether text messaging can enhance parents' involvement in their children's education.

Perhaps most encouraging of all has been the explosion of social networking in education, as teachers take to services like Facebook and Twitter to develop their own professional and personal learning networks to share good practice and collaborate with colleagues. The results are there for anyone to see by simply checking out Twitter hashtags (search terms), like #ukedchat, #edchat, #edtech and #hwbdysgu and #addcym (organised by educators in Wales). And schools and school leaders are also accepting the value of social networking.

When this online activity is integrated with events like education conferences and informal 'unconferences' such as TeachMeets, the effect has been to spread the ideas and learning in ways previously unimaginable. In fact, some extremely effective education events, like the Expeditionary Learning event featuring US educator Ron Berger for XP School (see 'Looking for inspiration? Make your school the source'),[24] have been organised on the back of a single tweet.

The social networking also helps educators keep abreast of the daunting rate of change in technology, where products that have not even been used yet are, worryingly, often hailed as 'the next big thing', and the statistics are even more dramatic than those in education. A quick look at market analyst Gartner's predictions, released in January 2014, gives an idea of the scale (Reuters).[25]

Gartner expects the combined global shipments of all digital devices in 2014 to reach 2.48 billion units, 7.6 per cent up on 2013. Although it anticipates Apple selling 344 million new devices, from phones to computers (up 28 per cent), Android is expected to sell 26 per cent more – 1.1 billion! Even Microsoft, which was late to the tablet market, is forecast to see its Windows in 360 million new devices, up from 326 million in 2013.

Gartner confirms the drift from desktop PCs to tablets, sales of which were expected to increase by 47 per cent overall to 263 million in 2014. Gartner research director Ranjit Atwal said, 'Users continue to move away from the traditional PC as it becomes more of a shared-content creation tool, while the greater flexibility of tablets, hybrids and lighter notebooks address users' increasingly different usage demands.'

Of course the statistics for the big hitters don't reflect the surprise successes, like Chromebooks, the light, cheap laptops based on Google's Chrome operating system. According to TechCrunch (using data from NPD Group), these accounted for 21 per cent of laptop sales in the USA in 2013. Many are believed to have gone into schools (they are also part of a major programme in Malaysia).[26]

With such major market shifts there is a premium on advice, which is why we have included a section on implementation (see Chapter 1). And it's just as well that the UK has no shortage of educators who can look back to earlier days, and lessons learned, and temper the excitement with experience, common sense and reminders to focus on the learning. Like consultant Ray Barker, who experienced success with mobile devices in London primary schools back in the 1990s.

Ray Barker says, 'My mantra always was, "If it's not the tool for the task, then don't use it. Don't be seduced by the technology".' His '4 Es' for working with technology are:

1. Does it ease and support the task in hand?

2. Does it enable the learner?

3. Does it ensure that learning outcomes are achieved?

4. Does it enhance the quality and value of the task?

Dave Whyley, using feedback from the Learning2Go project, provides even more to think about. 'Put mobile technology into a didactic, class-based learning scenario and it will have little impact. It would be better and cheaper to use pencil and paper,' he said.

> Mobile learning is all about enabling the following characteristics, but above all the students need to be able to move around with the devices and learn with them wherever they are. Mobile learning is NOT sitting in a classroom with every child with a device just searching the internet . . . or taking notes . . .

The key components of effective mobile learning are:

- Learners choose the learning content and applications.
- Learners use applications to 'manage' their learning.
- Learners integrate artefacts, objects, and real experiences that surround their daily lives (real world learning).
- Learners move around with the device and are motivated to expand the learning outside the classroom walls.
- Learners work collaboratively to explore the world around them.
- Learners are motivated to search for several possible options, solutions and answers to problems.
- Learners are presented with extended project-based learning.

- Learners keep the devices all of the time and 'own them'.
- Learners engage with 'authentic' learning experiences.
- Learners blend 'class time' and 'their own time' without realising it.
- The device bridges between home and school to engage parents in their children's learning.

   Teachers can manage and view the work on the device – workflow and assessment are important.

It's increasingly important for educators to remain focused on the learning, and with their feet on the ground, because the pace of technological change is not slowing. And there is no shortage of highly speculative technology coverage masquerading as confident predictions for the future of learning and teaching.

   What we already know provides sufficient challenges. It's a microchip maelstrom. If schools in developing countries already consider mobile phones a disruption, how will they cope with wearable technologies like Google Glass? And in developing countries they might be sufficiently free of techno-baggage to take fresher approaches as resources become available.

Notes

1 *Daily Mail.* Every School Child in Los Angeles to Get an iPad. www.dailymail.co.uk/news/article-2345124/EVERY-school-child-Los-Angeles-iPad-state-strikes-30m-deal-Apple.html (accessed 14 July 2014).
2 Znet.com. Malaysia Adopts Google Apps, Chromebooks for Education. www.zdnet.com/my/malaysia-adopts-google-apps-chromebooks-for-education-7000013847/ (accessed 14 July 2014).
3 *Metro.* Kent School Gives an iPad to Each of Its 1,400 Pupils. http://metro.co.uk/2011/07/14/kent-school-gives-an-ipad-to-each-of-its-1400-pupils-77258/ (accessed 14 July 2014).
4 Cuban, L (2013) A Second Look at iPads in Los Angeles. http://larrycuban.wordpress.com/2013/12/06/a-second-look-at-ipads-in-los-angeles/ (accessed 14 July 2014).
5 Learning Without Frontiers: www.learningwithoutfrontiers.com/ (accessed 14 July 2014).
6 McFarlane, A, Roche, N & Triggs, P (2007) *Mobile Learning: Research Findings.* Report to Becta. http://dera.ioe.ac.uk/1470/1/becta_2007_mobilelearning_interim_report.pdf (accessed 14 July 2014).
7 The report of the Docklands Learning Acceleration Project is only available as a hard copy. Unesco case study: http://www.unesco.org/education/lwf/doc/portfolio/case2.htm (accessed 14 July 2014).
   More on Docklands project in Leask, M & Meadows J (eds) (2000) *Teaching and Learning with ICT in the Primary School.* London: Routledge Falmer.
   And Scott, D & Usher, R (1999) *Researching Education.* London: Institute of Education. See www.ioe.ac.uk/staff/cpat/lccn_74.html (accessed 14 July 2014); www.bloomsbury.com/author/robin-usher (accessed 14 July 2014).

8 Learning2Go: www.wolverhampton-engage.net/sites/anonymous/Learning2Go/ Pages/default.aspx (accessed 14 July 2014).

9 E-scape: www.gold.ac.uk/teru/projectinfo/projecttitle,5882,en.php (accessed 14 July 2014).

   E-scape is now being marketed as ACJ and LiveAssess: www.tagassessment.com/acj (accessed 14 July 2014); www.tagassessment.com/liveassess (accessed 14 July 2014).

10 Agent4change.net. World's First EDA for Schools. http://agent4change.net/resources/ hardware/57 (accessed 14 July 2014).

11 Essa Academy: www.essaacademy.org/ (accessed 14 July 2014).

12 Normanby Primary School: www.redcar-cleveland.gov.uk/normanbyprimary (accessed 14 July 2014).

   Normanby headteacher Carl Faulkner won the Primary Practitioner Award at the Handheld Learning Awards 2009 while the school's PDAs to Support Learning Initiative took the Primary Innovation Award.

13 Cramlington Learning Village: www.cramlingtonlv.co.uk/ (accessed 14 July 2014).

14 Tablets for Schools: www.tabletsforschools.org.uk/ (accessed 14 July 2014).

15 Becta (Wikipedia): http://en.wikipedia.org/wiki/Becta (accessed 14 July 2014).

16 Gove speech to BETT 2012: www.gov.uk/government/speeches/michael-gove-speech-at-the-bett-show-2012 (accessed 14 July 2014).

17 Computing curriculum for English schools: www.gov.uk/government/publications/ national-curriculum-in-england-computing-programmes-of-study (accessed 14 July 2014).

   BCS – The Chartered Institute for IT: www.bcs.org/ (accessed 14 July 2014).

   Royal Academy of Engineering: www.raeng.org.uk/ (accessed 14 July 2014).

18 BESA (British Educational Suppliers Association). *Procurement in Authority, Schools and Academies, Part 1: View from Schools.* www.besa.org.uk/library?title=&field_document_ type_tid=211 (accessed 14 July 2014); www.besa.org.uk/ (accessed 14 July 2014).

19 e-Learning Foundation: www.e-learningfoundation.com/ (accessed 14 July 2014).

20 Littler, M (2014) Touch and Pads Open Door to SEN 'Dream Device'. Agent4change. net. http://agent4change.net/inclusion/inclusion/2106 (accessed 14 July 2014).

21 Burden, K, Hopkins, P, Male, M, Martin, S & Trala, C (Faculty of Education, The University of Hull). *iPad Scotland Evaluation.* www2.hull.ac.uk/ifl/ipadresearchinschools. aspx (accessed 14 July 2014).

22 Fullan, M & Langworthy, M (2013) *New Pedagogies for Deep Learning.* www. michaelfullan.ca/wp-content/uploads/2013/08/New-Pedagogies-for-Deep-Learning-An-Invitation-to-Partner-2013–6–201.pdf (accessed 14 July 2014).

23 Nominet Trust: www.nominettrust.org.uk/news-events/news/schools-to-test-whether-ipads-texting-and-technology-can-improve-results (accessed 14 July 2014); Education Endowment Foundation: http://educationendowmentfoundation.org.uk/ about (accessed 14 July 2014).

24 Agent4change.net: Looking for Inspiration? Make Your School the Source. http:// agent4change.net/innovation/innovation/2073 (accessed 14 July 2014).

25 Gartner predictions for 2014 (Reuters): www.reuters.com/article/2014/01/07/ us-mobile-devices-gartner-idUSBREA060E220140107 (accessed 14 July 2014); www.gartner.com/technology/home.jsp (accessed 14 July 2014).

26 TechCrunch (2013) Google's Chromebooks Have Hit Their Stride. http://techcrunch. com/2013/12/28/googles-chromebooks-have-hit-their-stride/ (accessed 14 July 2014).

1 Implementation

Deciding that handheld and portable devices will benefit your learners is probably quite an easy decision to make. Deciding which device, or devices, to invest in, then introducing them into your school will doubtless prove more challenging.

For a start there are so many to choose from, with more coming on to the market all the time. While the iPad is currently the market leader, it certainly isn't the only tablet around, and its lead is being challenged by several others joining the race, particularly when it comes to schools.

Tablets emerged as personal devices, a way for individuals to organise their lives, connect with friends and family, making their photos, music and videos available wherever and whenever they wanted. Schools quickly saw their potential to provide online content easily to students and young people, and to give them tools for responding and making their own. However, fitting a personal device into an institutional situation has brought many challenges. Despite this, schools are increasingly keen to bring highly mobile technologies into the classroom, and with them the possibilities for a greater range of innovative approaches to teaching and learning.

What to buy?

There are plenty of devices to choose from, and many more becoming available, so today's decision might not hold good in a year's time when the next tranche of funding comes through. In the less than 5 years that the iPad has been around, it has had three different iterations and a smaller version now exists. Where once the BlackBerry dominated the mobile phone market, it is now struggling to survive. And Windows 8 could be a game changer as it aims to demonstrate that one operating system can operate on all devices – laptop, desktop, tablet and phone.

What to buy could have a different answer every time the question is asked.

Do some research

While there is plenty of choice, then, there are also plenty of ways of getting the information you need to make a well-considered choice. While you might already have an idea of what you want, it's always good to check your decisions and gather some intelligence.

For a start there is your own experience, and that of your colleagues, pupils, governors and parents. Smartphones aren't uncommon (51 per cent of adults and 66 per cent of teenagers have them, according to Ofcom),[1] with some phones already looking like small tablets ('phablets'), and tablets themselves are increasingly used at home and work. Users often have an opinion about their devices: ask for it, find out what people like and dislike and why. It may be unscientific, but their views can demonstrate trends that reveal unexpected strengths and weaknesses.

Some colleagues will be key to the success of using handhelds and mobiles in school. The technical support staff will have to implement your decision, and deal with any issues that arise. Involving them at an early stage can help prevent problems. They will be able to help with the specification of devices, such as memory needs, processor speeds or network connection.

Learning support and special needs departments are also worth talking to. Some devices will work better than others for different kinds of learning difficulties, or have more appropriate built-in accessibility tools, or a more inclusive interface. Touchscreens don't work for all children so some peripherals, even just a selection of styli, might be needed.

Objective external advice is important, especially following the axing of the Government's own educational ICT agency, Becta, by the Coalition Government. A local-authority ICT adviser (if your area still has one) should know about these things, and be able to direct you to sources of useful information. Or one of the ICT-focused professional associations such as Naace[2] (a national UK membership organisation for those involved in learning with technology) might be able to suggest someone who can help.

There are also blogs and sites run by experts and academics. Professor Peter Twining of the Open University runs the EdFutures[3] 'bliki' (a cross between a blog and wiki), which is packed with helpful information and advice.

There are also campaigning organisations, like the e-Learning Foundation[4] and Tablets for Schools,[5] which should be able to provide appropriate advice in the context of their own campaigns. Tablets for Schools supporter 9ine Consulting was involved in one of the UK's first iPad 1:1 schemes at Longfield Academy and has produced a helpful Q&A advice paper which can be downloaded from the Tablets for Schools website.

Your school might have a preferred supplier, perhaps as part of a managed service, who can give you some advice, although you might have to judge how objective you think it is. Or you could seek out advice from consultants who have worked on successful school projects incorporating mobile technology. The better ones ought to be able to resist commercial influences to give you professional advice based on your own aims and hopes.

Similarly, there are plenty of shops where sales staff will be only too happy to run through their range of stock, although they are not likely to have much experience of 'enterprise solutions'. A more considered view might be gleaned from comparison sites, such as Which?[6] or Techradar.[7]

The most important question is what can be achieved with mobile technologies, and that's best found out from those already using them. Schools already using tablets are often generous with their advice; some host their own open days and many of them are featured in case studies (such as those later in this book). There are others on company websites or on blogs and forums — for an objective view, try education-focused websites such as *TES*[8] or agent4change.net.[9]

How to buy?

There are a number of approaches to purchasing tablets, which can roughly be summed up as follows.

- One is the carefully considered approach, determining what aspects of teaching and learning tablets will support, and then finding a device that meets those requirements and is manageable.

- Another is the piloting or 'suck it and see' method, where a limited number of devices are purchased and tested before a decision is taken about what role they could play across the curriculum and, therefore, how many to buy and where to deploy them.

- A third, not seriously recommended, way is to follow the trend and invest in tablets, then work out why! (On a serious note, some respected observers say that just starting the 1:1 process can stimulate the kinds of discussion that can lead to breakthroughs for learning.)

Whichever route you take, the machines on offer will have various features and functions to take into account. Whether or not these are what you need for teaching and learning in your establishment will help inform your decision.

There are more questions than answers

While the most important consideration in choosing which devices are best for your school is how they will be used in teaching and learning, you may well start by considering how well they are built. For example, which would perform and stand up to wear better in your classroom — a Tesco Hudl, an iPad mini or a Microsoft Surface RT? And then there is how much you can afford to spend.

Things to consider

Deployment

Will these be individual devices that each pupil has responsibility for, perhaps even providing their own as part of a BYOD (bring your own device – see below) implementation? Are they for individual use and ownership or will they be shared, either issued to each class or subject, or as groups of machines centrally held and booked out for lessons?

While the 1:1 route is attractive, giving your learners equality of access, it has a considerable overhead. In some instances schools have been able to bring it about through initiatives such as Building Schools for the Future.[10] Here they decided to use the exceptional influx of funding to kick-start a level of technology provision that would not ordinarily be possible. In other instances schools have decided that this level of resourcing is essential and have asked families to help, either by buying devices or through a rental or leasing scheme. Such arrangements can prove controversial, especially when additional costs such as connectivity away from school, installation of apps, insurance and replacement are taken into account.

In order to ensure equity, purchase of machines for students from less well-off families may need to be partly, or wholly, subsidised by the school. This is an area where additional funding, such as the Pupil Premium[11] funds (around £900 per pupil in 2013), can be used. However, the question of connectivity away from school will still be an issue, one that might be addressed through the provision of pay-as-you-go dongles[12] or subscription for internet access. A home/school agreement will be needed to determine who is responsible for what – particularly in case of loss, theft or damage. Specific arrangements for insurance cover could be useful.

Funding

This is possibly the most crucial question. What is there to spend currently? How can it be sustained in the future so that this initiative is more than a one-off project? Who else can help? Should parents be asked to supplement purchases? The cheapest tablets can cost a quarter of the price of the most expensive ones. Can cost be balanced against functionality and performance? What about ongoing costs such as support and insurance? How long does the warranty last? What does it cover? Does it matter if all students have the same devices? The e-Learning Foundation has advised on many school projects and should be a good source of up-to-date information.

Using learners' own devices

With the ubiquity of smartphone ownership, secondary schools are increasingly coming to realise that most students already carry around a powerful computer in their pockets, so why not make use of them – with bring your own device (BYOD)? With this approach, rather than provide computers for students, the school will provide a wireless infrastructure that students can then access with their own machines which are registered for students on the school network. While this is attractive for the school in terms of cost and sustainability, there are issues of network vulnerability, file and data management, and online safety. (With BYOT, bring your own technology, which is considered by many to be more appealing to students, devices don't have to be registered so young people can use whatever technology they happen to be using at the time.)

Replacement

Questions of ownership also raise concerns about who is responsible for replacing the device, either because of theft or accident, or through the need to upgrade. Who insures it? Is it on the school's asset register? Is the value such that any excess on the policy makes a claim pointless? Are these devices ultimately consumables?

Operating systems

There are a few operating systems that dominate the mobile and handheld market. Apple devices use iOS, first introduced in 2007 when it set the standard for tablet computers. Google's Android is now well established, although Chromebooks (netbook devices where most of the applications and files are held on the internet, not the computer, and are accessed via a browser) use the Chrome operating system. BlackBerry uses its own operating system on some devices, and more recently Android on others. Then there is Microsoft's Windows 8. This is designed to look and work in the same way, seamlessly, across all Windows devices. So whether it's a PC, smartphone or tablet, users will know how it operates and all their files and documents can be found, opened and saved in roughly the same way, with files being stored on the devices or on Microsoft's own online space, which is free to schools.

Operating systems are in a constant state of flux, with new ones entering the market or older ones being upgraded. While consistency is helpful, particularly for those with a range of special needs and disabilities, generally speaking people (especially young ones) are more adaptable. And whichever operating system the devices run will have advantages and drawbacks. Functionality and price will probably decide which device you go with rather than what operating system it runs unless your investment is such that it might not be cost-effective to switch.

Battery life

Can the device survive a complete school day without a recharge? How can it be recharged? And who is responsible? Do you need extra charging points – perhaps built into student lockers? Or charging trolleys?

Storage

How will devices be kept secure? Will pupils be required to carry them around? Will there be bulk storage facilities for class groups of machines, or can individuals put them on charge in their lockers? Can class teachers lock them away safely? Will they be security-etched? Or can the screens be watermarked in some way so that their ownership is obvious and indisputable?

Protection

Is the device robust enough to survive the rigours of a school environment? Will cases be issued for all students? Or does the device require extra protection? A rugged case perhaps, or a screen cover?

Productivity/creativity

Will students mainly use the machine as consumers of information? Or will they also be creators? If so, what types of file will they be producing? Audio – sound or music? Image – video, photos or graphics? Text – with a keyboard, or using speech-to-text? If devices are shared, can individuals use unique log-ins, and create and save work without causing confusion for others? Or do protocols have to be established for file management?

Data storage

Does the device have sufficient memory to store all the work created on it safely? Or is there a need to move work off to be stored elsewhere? Can this be done through the network? Or on online services like Google Drive, Office365/OneDrive or Dropbox? Can storage be expanded through the use of SD cards, or USB memory sticks? If not, can work be stored in the cloud? Will users need individual accounts for cloud services, or can class ones suffice?

Screen quality

Does it matter how crisp and clear the content displayed on the tablet is? Will it be used for watching videos, or viewing photos? Is the resolution sufficient for the job? Is it big enough to view content, or do tasks become fiddly because space is too tight? How responsive is the touch technology? Is it fast, responsive and accurate, or slow and frustratingly inaccurate? Will users need a stylus, particularly adults with thicker fingers or children with poor fine-motor control?

Size

How portable does the device need to be? Can it be easily carried? Or operated with one hand and held with the other? Will pupils find it awkward to operate if it is either too large or too small for different tasks? Will on-screen content be easily discernible on a small screen?

Sound

Will pupils need to listen to music or voice recordings? If so, how clear does the audio need to be? Will it vary between subjects? And between pupils? Can they manage using headphones?

Sound recording

Will users need a microphone? To record themselves? Or music? Or for video conferencing? Or as part of creating multimedia work? Can an external microphone be added to improve sound quality?

Cameras

Is it necessary to have a camera to produce photos or video, or to use for video conferencing? What level of quality does the camera need? Does it need a user-facing camera for video conferencing? Or just a forward-facing one for taking photos of work? Or two cameras, one facing each way? If it doesn't have one, would it be workable to add one via a USB port?

Connectivity

The machine has to be compatible with the school network. Does it need to have internet connectivity at all times in all places, perhaps needing 3G or 4G too, or will wifi suffice? Is the device dependent on an internet connection to be fully functional? Will users have sufficient rights to connect to wifi hotspots outside school?

App management

How will apps be provided? Centrally by technical support staff? Individually by users, whether students or teachers? A bit of both? And who's paying for them? How? Vouchers? Or personal or school credit cards? Site licences (i.e. bulk discounts) or their equivalent are essential.

Accessibility

The touch interface of tablets makes them more inclusive for many users with disabilities and special needs. Are there particular features designed to make the machine more accessible, such as speech-to-text, text-to-speech and a configurable interface? Will users with special needs find the tablets sufficiently accessible, or will they need a different device or a range of peripherals? Will the machine support additions such as Braille keyboards, or switches? Is the on-screen keyboard sufficient for student needs, or will students need additional keyboards, perhaps with wireless or Bluetooth connections?

In answering these questions you will need to do some research. You will need to know what your favoured device is meant to achieve for the school. Is it a tool for managers to improve efficiency? For pupils to raise achievement? In particular classes, such as art or music? Or every classroom for quick access to digital tools and online content? Or a combination of several things?

Making an informed decision will require working with stakeholders, members of the school community, including staff, pupils, governors and parents, who may already have something that's worth considering – like a smartphone, Kindle, Blackberry or iPad. Talking to them about the pros and cons of each will be a start. Visiting shops or exhibitions and getting some hands-on time will make tangible the specifications that are written in the advertising blurb. Some websites, such as Which?, offer comparison charts that can help narrow down the choice.

Remember to keep the technical support staff on board, too, consulting and updating them frequently, as they will have to make the whole initiative work, ensuring a smooth service and a swift response to any problems.

There are other members of the school community, too, who can help find solutions to potential difficulties. The bursar may have a view on insurance, warranties and adding devices to the asset register. Premises staff can assist with identifying points to keep the devices charged and ways of managing any additional energy needs. It helps to ensure that students have a sense of ownership of any rules regarding use as they are more likely to adhere to the rules, so involve them and the school council in drawing up policies for acceptable and responsible use.

Given the wide range of learning needs in a school, the differing contexts for use and the breadth of features and functions of devices, it is unlikely that any single device will meet all your criteria. While some schools have focused on one particular brand, others are developing a mixed economy, sometimes developing in an organic way, rather than sticking to a preplanned, strategic approach.

Managing machines

One of the key decisions in implementing any ICT initiative in schools is how machines will be managed, and by whom.

Some of the more technical aspects of this, such as network access or internet connectivity, will need to be dealt with by appropriately qualified support staff, but others, for instance procuring, installing and updating apps, could fall to teaching staff and even students. Be clear where responsibilities lie.

Less technical aspects, such as issuing devices, reporting problems, keeping them safe during the school day and making sure they are charged when needed, will require straightforward answers. Others, like providing apps and resources, saving and sharing files, printing or uploading material to a website and creating layers of permissions for different levels of access, are more complex.

One determining factor is the operating system installed in the devices you select. While it's always good to keep things simple where possible, Apple's iOS is regarded by some to be too locked down – very prescriptive in how apps are purchased and installed. Android and Windows are more open, offering wider routes to acquiring software and installing it. However, this openness might give an unwanted level of complexity to those who appreciate the straightforward approach of selecting and downloading from Apple's iTunes.

iPad

The enduringly popular iPad was designed as a consumer device, a personal tool for individual use rather than an institutional one for shared or group use, yet it is increasingly in demand in the classroom. However, this central element of its conceptualisation has provided some challenges to its implementation in schools – not least trying to squeeze them into a closed-down, establishment-led, tightly controlled model for their management. However, this challenge is being addressed by schools and the resources Apple and third-party suppliers are offering.

In many ways a tablet could be conceived as an extension of the individual. It might have personal choices of music or film, memories of occasions encapsulated in photos or video, and quick access to tools to organise our lives, with diary, contacts and email. In this increasingly connected world it provides a means to share our thoughts and experiences immediately through Twitter, YouTube, Facebook or Google+, uploading images or passing on items of interest, with email as handy as SMS. The speed of operation means questions are quickly answered online, or news and entertainment brought instantly to hand, with the screen quality making it all crisp, bright and easy to see, and sound that is good enough to share, and easy to enhance with headphones. What's not to like? Critics would offer a number of points.

For a start there is the way in which the management of content and apps is locked into iTunes. Users need an account which will helpfully offer to incorporate all their existing media into the device management process. With no USB ports, file transfer is managed either through the 'cloud', in particular the iCloud facility automatically provided with the device, or by connecting the iPad to a conventional computer – preferably an Apple. Similarly, there is no slot for an SD card, so photos or contacts can't be quickly transferred from storage on a camera or smartphone. Although there is the Airdrop facility from IOS7 onwards that wirelessly connects users, this is something that schools may want to restrict to ensure sharing doesn't become copying or cheating.

File management can also be more convoluted than with other devices because of the use of iTunes, and the lack of a drag-and-drop facility on the machine itself. Music, documents and video just don't move around as simply as with other systems. There is also a problem with retrieving deleted files as there is no wastebasket, so no safety net for getting accidentally removed content back again – which could be crucial where devices are shared in school and multiple users are creating files, in art or music for instance.

The lack of USB can also frustrate when adding peripheral devices such as keyboards or printers, and necessitates using bespoke Apple connectors for this purpose, or using Bluetooth or wireless. This might not always be difficult, but it can make existing add-ons redundant. Also absent is a slot for an HDMI lead to connect to a TV. Apple provides solutions – such as Apple TV or a bespoke lead – but generic cables you already own would be simpler.

A mouse is one peripheral that is missing as everything is driven by touch. But for very detailed or accurate work, when 'painting' for instance, it can be better to use a stylus, and similarly if the user has problems with fine-motor control, a hand tremor or particularly thick fingers. Likewise the on-screen keyboard invites users to hunt and peck; as it is not tactile it doesn't lend itself to touch typing so is much slower. There are, of course, solutions to this, with Bluetooth keyboards available, or protective cases with them built-in, but essay writing isn't something iPads were designed for, although it is a regular task in schools.

Managing apps is one issue that Apple has begun to address. Everything has to go through iTunes and Apple takes a percentage of the price; even if developers want to give their product away, there is a fee payable to Apple.

From one perspective this streamlines and simplifies the whole system. However, it is designed for a consumer purchasing resources for personal use and can cause problems elsewhere. The licensing arrangements are such that apps are intended to be bought for individual use, with one purchaser being able to install each one on all the devices he or she owns, usually to a maximum of five. In schools this has often been translated as one purchase covering five devices, although this is not in the spirit of the licensing agreement.

With devices that are shared, either a machine allocated to a class or a group of machines that can be booked out for particular activities, then one licence per iPad is necessary to be within the absolute letter of the licensing agreement. This has now been simplified with Apple's volume licensing arrangements whereby apps attract a discount when more than 20 licences are bought, but not all schools are happy with how that arrangement works.

iPad management has also been aided on a technical level with the use of software such as Apple Configurator or OS X Server, which enables multiple devices to be managed simultaneously, rather than a laborious one-at-a-time approach. Other aids to bulk device management are the range of storage devices and trolleys that will securely store, charge and sync machines.

Despite the view that the method for loading and managing apps on an iPad is pretty much a given, they can be set up to offer a continuum of installation and ownership choices.

The nuances of the various deployment options can be explored through the use of specialist advisers such as Linda Merrills of Inovaris (www.inovaris.co.uk), who guides schools through the complexities that Apple licensing can bring, and the less-than-obvious pitfalls that might be waiting. Could what might be seen as standard security procedures result in unwanted consequences?

Linda Merrills outlines three models of iPad deployment, structured around by whom and how apps are managed: personal, layered and institutional.

Personal

The personal approach hands responsibility over to users. They set up their own iTunes accounts for their allocated devices, then either pay for apps themselves or redeem school-issued gift vouchers for downloads. This is the nearest model to what Apple had in mind when it developed the product. It has the advantage of putting technical and operational considerations into the hands of the person who can respond quickest, and who has the greatest interest in sorting them out. No need to wait for anyone's approval before buying and installing a new resource. Which is also a disadvantage, as control over what resources are available is given to individuals. This might not present value for money, it could be inappropriate or it might not have any use in the classroom at all and be solely for the user's personal enjoyment.

Layered

A layered approach offers a 'mixed-economy' model whereby the school provides the device and a core set of apps, then users adds their own selection to it. Each machine running the IOS operating system can work with up to five iTunes accounts, meaning that a system manager can retain installation rights, and class teachers, or pupils, can add apps specific to their needs.

Organising such arrangements can mean working a little differently to the iPad norm, with dummy email addresses and iTunes accounts without credit cards allocated to them, so it needs to be well structured and closely managed from the outset. However, such a system allows for both a degree of central oversight of how devices are configured, with uniform suites of tools on every machine, alongside flexibility across classrooms, subjects and users.

Institutional

The advent of multi-user licensing, coupled with tools for managing many devices such as Apple Configurator, and the introduction of cases, trolleys and boxes for bulk storage and synchronisation has made an institutional management approach easier. Technicians can create backup images of machines so any rebuilding can happen quickly, bursars can more easily log purchases, and departments can manage apps just as they do with other resources.

The bulk licensing system requires establishments to purchase a set number of apps – more than 20 – for which a discount is given. The school records the licence numbers of each app, but only has to sync any one of them to the given number of iPads. Along with Apple Configurator, this licensing shifts the conceptualisation of the iPad from individual to institutional use. Problems of shifting files between pupils and teachers remain, but it is fairly easy to train everyone to use facilities such as iCloud or Dropbox[13] for this purpose.

The quick emergence of the iPad in the marketplace as well as its slick design and obvious quality have given it a lead as the desirable device when it comes to tablets, but its intended role as a lifestyle gadget can make its transition into an institutional one a complex affair. It's important to remember that there are alternatives.

Android

Android is an operating system that runs on tablets and smartphones available from many different producers, unlike the iPad, which is a device and an operating system specific only to Apple. Android is also an operating system that can be adapted by developers to create their own variations. One company that has taken advantage of this is Avantis, which started working from the perspective of how schools might want to use tablets, and what the implications are for managing them.

Avantis created the LearnPad, a tablet with the Android operating system underpinning it, with schools and classrooms, teachers and learners in mind. The result is in many ways very similar to the iPad, and in others quite different. It is also considerably more affordable.

The similarities are a good-quality screen, with front- and rear-facing cameras, built-in microphone and speakers, an accelerometer to reorient it depending on how it is being held and built-in wifi. The LearnPad then adds Micro USB and HDMI ports for connectivity, and a slot for an SD card for external storage. (As it is based on Android, the software can run on any device also using that operating system; it is not restricted to Avantis' bespoke tablet.)

In many respects what you can do with it is pretty much the same as the iPad, too – accessing information, creating content, using simulations, playing games, exploring virtual models, connecting and communicating with others, and viewing and listening to films and audio.

The most significant difference is in the way that it is managed. The LearnPad design began from the perspective that its use would be organised by teachers in classrooms, so teachers need control of what's available through it. One perceived problem with tablets, or indeed any computer in schools, is that children and young people can wander off task. When they should be preparing a presentation on the metamorphosis of the caterpillar they might be sneaking a peek at the team sheet for that evening's match, or the latest travails of the inhabitants of the Big Brother House, or sharing their deepest thoughts on Facebook. While filtering and monitoring help to reduce the opportunities for such behaviour, the fun that can be had with tablets extends beyond websites to the apps themselves. Pupils don't need to be online to find something to absorb and distract – as even the most diligent of us have probably experienced ourselves.

With this in mind Avantis developed a system, also called LearnPad, where resources – whether apps, websites, documents or online content – are brought together into what they refer to as Profiles. When learners are working they are restricted to the content of the Profile. Some tools, such as cameras, sound recorders, Notepad and so on – the ones needed to create or to respond to an activity – can be made available at all times; others are only loaded for specific subjects or lessons. While there may be a common set of resources for curriculum subjects, instrument simulators in music for instance, or a set-up for history which includes BBC history pages and the British Museum Compass site, there may also be a set for specific topics, such as Florence Nightingale, or baroque composers.

While the device comes with some such sets provided, mainly free online resources and open-source apps, they are intended to be managed by teachers. Online cloud storage is provided wherein staff create Profiles then associate them with a quick response (QR) code[14] (these are the small black squares, something like barcodes, which are often seen on advertising or packaging). When a camera on a tablet or smartphone is pointed at the QR code, it triggers a response which is usually to open a website. In this instance, when the camera on the LearnPad is pointed at the QR code the teacher has created, it is to change the set of apps, the Profile. What was previously a device ready to study one subject, art perhaps, is now set up to be used for another, such as English.

A similar method can be used for other actions. To download student work – photos they may have taken, for instance – a QR code can be used to retrieve them from the device and save them into a specific folder.

Because the machine is connected to the school network, file management is much the same as on any other computer in the school. Folders and their contents can be seen, documents uploaded, downloaded and moved around. The LearnPad is intended to be used with cloud storage, so apps and documents can also be accessed through the internet.

Flexibility is also gained through the ports provided, so peripherals such as keyboards and printers can be directly attached, or content saved or uploaded either through the USB connection or on and off an SD card.

Like the iPad there are different sizes available, including a 13-inch version, as well as options for displaying the tablet's screen on the interactive whiteboard. The LearnPad has a built-in feature so the teacher can control all the machines in the class, to share their screens for instance, to see how pupils are getting on with the task, or to control all the tablets in the class, locking them so all present have to focus on what is being said, or pushing fresh content to everyone. (This can be brought about on the iPad by downloading an app such as Nearpod.)

The LearnPad does not have quite the high design quality of the iPad, but it has been created from a functional perspective, that of the classroom, trying to give the benefits that a tablet brings while offering a degree of control that may help teachers feel confident that their charges are doing what they should be doing, and not wandering off on an undirected course of learning.

The LearnPad is by no means the only Android tablet used in classrooms. It is effectively providing a shell within which teachers and classes can work, and the LearnPad management software will run on any of these devices from other manufacturers (and can now also manage iPads and Windows devices).

Even without the LearnPad framework, other Android devices offer similar options for managing devices, connecting to networks and online storage, moving files between them and so on without being constrained by specific routines.

Others may see those routines as simplifying life, ensuring everything happens smoothly by channelling activities in one preset, easily managed, direction.

Windows 8

Despite being a late entry into the tablet arena, devices running Windows 8 as an operating system will no doubt prove attractive. They are trying to offer not so much an adjunct to a lifestyle, but more of a device for productive tasks that bridges a gap between what we have long expected our computers to do, and the essential extension of our personal way of life they have recently afforded us with their easy portability.

There are two versions of Windows 8 depending upon the capacity of the device it is installed on. More powerful ones run a version that includes the desktop view option of a typical Windows computer.

Essentially these can be fully functioning hybrid laptops where you can separate the screen from the keyboard to make it a tablet, and run it with the appropriate version of the operating system. Rather like switching between the tiled view that is standard in this version – what Microsoft refers to as the Metro or Modern Style UI (user interface) – and the classic Windows view. On lower-specification tablets, using the ARM processor, Windows RT is used. This effectively uses the tablet interface, although with a version of the standard desktop available.

To avoid confusion, the RT is to a Windows computer what the iPad is to a desktop Mac – not fully compatible, but with a more closely aligned appearance and way of working. A full Windows 8 tablet should give a user more or less the same functions as a desktop Windows computer.

There is an argument that this degree of choice can cause confusion, even though the overall intention is to provide an operating system that gives users the same experience regardless of the device they are working on.

When coupled with file management that is uniform throughout, and cloud storage space designed to coordinate storage so the activity becomes the focus rather than where, when and on what they are accessed, this could present an option that is the best of both worlds. A personal device that gives access to whatever media is desired whenever it is wanted, along with a way of working that is well established and familiar.

The full version of Windows 8 on a tablet runs everything as any other computer, while the Windows RT variation has an Office app that works in the same way as its fully fledged cousin – although with some loss of functionality.

For many years Windows has been the operating system that has driven computers in British schools and such familiarity provides an attraction in working with a known system. So although the technology might be new, the way of working and networking, and possibly the activities undertaken, builds on what is already known and established. And there are no issues of compatibility.

File management is understood, and any curriculum content the school already uses (including Flash materials), or wishes to use in the future, will be available. Printing will also be straightforward as existing network procedures can continue as before.

Depending on the version of Windows 8 installed, any Microsoft program that will run on any other machine in the school will be available, or a version of it. These devices are able to have multiple applications running, with two on show at any one time on the desktop, with interaction between them – although with some quirks, such as two different versions of Internet Explorer, one for each of the two variations of desktop – classic or Metro/Modern Style UI.

Questions of file management and installation of applications are likely to be easily answered too, as schools will see tablet uptake as an extension of existing provision and therefore technical support can continue to reside where it always has, with the tech support staff who are all familiar with Windows.

However, this familiarity could also have a downside. Tablets have been causing a stir in schools because they are acting as a spur to changing practice. Easy access to materials wherever students are located, along with the possibilities of sharing and collaborating, and having engaging creative tools immediately at hand might remain untapped and undiscovered because the impetus to change is missed. Established pedagogies will continue on new technology. Not in itself a bad thing, but staff and students might find themselves wondering what all the fuss around learning with handheld and mobile technologies is about.

Likewise, an opportunity could be missed to shift some of the technical tasks, such as selecting and installing apps, from the support team to the users. A culture of dependency, and of unfulfilled expectations, could continue.

There are a number of manufacturers who are using Windows 8, or Windows RT, as the operating system for their tablets, so there is a degree of choice around what to buy, which should keep the market competitive. They are all being developed with the ability to attach peripherals such as keyboards and mice through USB, and to connect to printers or large displays and TV screens, as well as external storage. Bluetooth is a standard and keyboards built into protective covers are also universally available.

While Android and Apple are well established in the handheld market, it is very likely that Microsoft won't take long to catch up. The late entry means that others are ahead of the field in terms of apps, but the opportunities that it opens up won't be ignored by developers. With their historical market-leading position in software in schools, it is very likely many of the titles already established in UK education will be refashioned for Windows 8 and Windows RT.

Google Chromebooks

One of the more radical interventions in the mobile technology market has been the Google Chromebook. This is essentially a netbook but stripped down to very little hardware as almost everything is sitting online in the cloud and accessible through a browser (essentially the Chrome operating system is a browser). The advantage is that most of the tools used are free and constantly improving; the disadvantage is the necessity for a reliable internet connection. (In fact, the device does have some storage and can hold files, even movies, on SD cards.)

Most of the resources will also be hosted online, with the exception of any apps downloaded from Google's Play Store. Once users have a profile, it is then just a case of logging on to the machine to get access to their files and resources from within the cloud. As each Chromebook can cope with several individual log-ins, they are devices that can be shared, but all users can have a unique set of tools and materials which are held securely for them.

Being stripped of many internal workings means that Chromebooks are light and easy to use. They may not have the allure of tablets or smartphones but they are portable and have a long battery life, so can be used anywhere. In addition, there is the bonus of an integral keyboard equipped for writing and working with text in a way that other highly portable devices are not. And as applications are not installed on the machines but accessed through the web, very little technical support is needed. If there is a problem with one machine, a user can simply log on to another and take up where he or she left off.

There is an attractive simplicity to this solution, particularly since the need for a reliable infrastructure that can cope with everyone being online all the time is increasingly in place in schools. There may be limitations in what the online apps can cope with – photo editing might lack sophistication without something like Photoshop to work with – but no one device will meet all the teaching and learning needs in schools anyway. For much of what children and young people do in schools, online tools such as Google Docs[15] and Pixlr will be sufficient.

BYOD

The attraction of the BYOD approach is clear. The obligation for providing technology for learning in schools, and therefore the cost, is shifted from institution to individual learners – well, their parents. The problem is twofold. One is the inconsistency of devices and applications that learners will bring; the other is that some of them won't be able to bring a device at all. The latter can be addressed in a number of ways, including: regular, low-cost, parental contributions over an extended period of time; using allocated funds such as the Pupil Premium; and leasing and loaning machines, all of which have been successfully used in UK schools, many of them supported by the e-Learning Foundation.

To make BYOD work, and to cope with the myriad devices that will accompany learners, schools need to be confident that their infrastructure is robust enough to allow hundreds of users access at all times in all places. They could be using devices with different operating systems to access their files and to get online, so the network needs to be secure, and also capable of allowing many levels of access. And students' own devices will only be part of the answer. While they can all do research and access learning resources, even on a smartphone, they might struggle to edit a video, create a presentation or author a book.

A number of factors come into play that make the BYOD option less straightforward than at first it seems, suggesting that schools may need to be quite prescriptive in what that device does. As well as viewing learning resources, students may be required to respond in some way, or create their own. Some materials may need particular software to run, such as Flash. The school's learning platform will need to be able to run in any browser, and on any operating system. Whatever the device is, it will need a minimum specification to handle apps and software requirements for lessons. Along with the continued need to provide some devices for specific subjects where specialist software is used, such as design work in design and technology, or photo editing in art, and composition in music, there remains the perennial question of funding.

Putting it into practice

Just as there are different choices around the technology, so there are too about how to introduce it into the classroom, ranging from a laissez-faire 'What do you think this does?' through a more structured 'Give it a go and tell us what you find out,' to a more directive 'We are now using this.'

In the first bracket are the staff of Frank Wise School in Banbury (see Chapter 9). The school has long been at the forefront of using technology in teaching and learning. Its staff found that the most effective way to develop their skills with it was to make it personal to them – to take the machines home and just to explore.

After initially buying and trialling iPod Touches, the leadership team were confident that the iPad would be a useful device to have in school. With that certainty in mind they provided three of the tablets to every class, with the expectation that teachers would take one for themselves to explore and determine how it could enhance learning for their particular pupils. Having issued them with a standard set of apps, each class was provided with an iTunes voucher to take on the management of the device and purchase whatever teachers and students felt was appropriate.

To support this approach, staff are encouraged to share their experiences at staff meetings, and one member of staff, a teaching assistant, has a specific brief to help with the use of technology in class.

A more structured approach was taken by Riverside School in Haringey when they began to introduce iPads into the school. This secondary special school is organised in both class groups and with some subjects taught by specialists. As such there weren't enough devices to go into every class, or to every subject specialist. The solution that ICT coordinator Ben Annett implemented was to add an edge of competition to determine who should be the first to get them. Teachers were challenged to put forward ideas for how they could be used, and what outcomes might be expected.

Suggestions ranged from broad aims to support existing learning activities to very specific ones for particular students. One idea was to record and play back science experiments, another to develop a design technology project on puppet making to include the Puppet Pals app, whereas in music and drama an iPad would provide sound effects and a video-recording device where students could more easily view what was being recorded. For individuals, ideas ranged from teaching hand and eye coordination to acting as a communication aid, providing images and activities to help calm a child down, and filming and playing back two of the pupils on the autistic spectrum to help them learn about emotions and responses.

A mixed group of staff, including teachers, therapists and teaching assistants, selected the projects to go ahead and the iPads were issued for the summer term, with a staff meeting given over at the end of term to reporting back. Structuring the introduction in this way meant that staff had something to focus on, rather than just experimenting and seeing where it would take them.

At Riverside it very quickly became obvious that the devices were having an impact, with staff swapping information and chatting about what they were up to, to the extent that even before the end of term more iPads had been bought and issued to other classes and staff.

In other schools the approach has been more highly structured, with a rapid shift from more traditional ways of working to technology-based ones, as at Essa Academy (see Chapter 6). Here a compelling case was made that not only would administrative and assessment tasks be more easily managed online, but also the distribution of learning resources to students, the setting and handing in of work, and communication between staff, and between students and staff, across the school. Not only are all textbooks and handouts now available electronically, but staff are using iBooks Author to create bespoke learning resources that are published for all the school to use and distributed through iTunes U.

The introduction of iPads was integral to a school shift towards a technology-based learning infrastructure, one that replaced many of the established ways of working with electronically based ones. This was not about tablets supplementing and enhancing classroom activity, but about becoming the fundamental tool for it.

One thing is sure: teachers need to be familiar with the technology before it is issued to the students and they have to cope with it, ready or not.

Safety – in all its forms

There are two broad aspects to safety when it comes to using handhelds and mobiles. One is to ensure that when children and young people are using highly portable devices they don't encounter content or users that might cause them distress, and that they in turn don't distress others. The other is to prevent the students from causing the devices to stop doing what they should, either through interfering with the software and settings, or by damaging them.

Keeping devices safe from students

This is the easier challenge to deal with, particularly the issue of causing physical damage such as breaking the screen. Buy one of the many cases and rigs that are on the market for just this purpose. As for ensuring that, for reasons of either malice aforethought or over-exuberant curiosity, the software and settings remain unchanged, there are means by which devices can be locked down. These vary between operating systems and brands.

The Android-based LearnPad has this built in as learners use QR codes to change sets of apps so they are limited to the tools and resources on offer, even down to specific websites, and can't wander freely (this is all configurable by the school). With iPads, designed with individuals in mind to set up as they please, a level of restriction will need to be introduced. Adults will want to keep many of the options out of harm's way, such as downloading or updating apps, adding content or extensions to them, deleting data, accepting messages and browsing inappropriate or offensive material.

Within the Settings widget are several options to make this possible. For a start there is an option under the General heading called Restrictions. Accessed with a user (staff)-defined pass code, here some fundamental capabilities can be turned off, including installing and deleting apps, using YouTube or Safari (the pre-installed internet browser) and FaceTime (the video-conferencing facility) and barring the use of explicit language when using voice-controlled features such as Siri, or when dictating.

Restrictions can also help filter some content by ratings, such as film categorisation, or explicit content in books and podcasts. Other settings prevent users from joining multiplayer games online, or from adding friends in those games.

Separately in the Settings area is the Messages area, where you can close down the facility to receive iMessages into the user's account.

Then there is the Guided Access option. This feature locks the iPad into a particular app that can only be changed through the use of a password. Within the app you can also set what buttons or areas of the screen are active by drawing masks over them; again these can only be modified after inputting a password.

Similar features are available in Windows 8. So, regardless of the operating system or manufacturer, controls can be put in place to limit users' access.

Keeping students safe online

In many respects keeping children safe when using handhelds and mobiles is no different from using any other device. When browsing the internet, school filtering systems will continue to block access to inappropriate content as tablets use the same browsers as computers, e.g. Internet Explorer, Safari, Firefox and Chrome.

The most effective protection remains, as always, in enabling children and young people to keep themselves safe, by teaching them to ensure confidential data remains private, including name, phone number, email and address, and by being wary that anyone they meet online might not be who they say they are. As always, if they encounter something that causes them distress or makes them anxious they need to tell someone.

Simple guidance such as only using a tablet or mobile where other people can see what they are up to, and having their browser history checked every so often also makes sure that learners know their activities online won't go unnoticed.

One way in which highly portable devices differ from other machines, such as laptops, desktops and gaming consoles, is just that – their ability to go anywhere. They are easy to conceal, so malicious or mischievous activities, such as filming people in difficult situations or acting in embarrassing ways, can be easily executed. Sports changing rooms, perhaps, or demonstrating moves in dance, or expressing personal thoughts and feelings can be captured and shared very quickly and easily.

The ways in which what could be distressing images and video can be shared and spread are diverse. Along with text messages there are sites such as Twitter, YouTube and Facebook, and tools such as Instagram so, whether deliberately or carelessly, an undesirable, damaging or distressing shot of someone can quickly make that person a victim of online amusement, embarrassment and derision.

This is particularly so in the case of sexting, where young people, especially girls, are persuaded to send self-taken sexually explicit images of themselves to others. Once an image is released on to the web it is very hard to control what happens to it, and no matter how much you trust someone, electronic media can be shared very easily.

Again the answer to much of this is esafety – teaching children and young people not to engage in behaviours that can cause problems for themselves or others. Schools' acceptable use policies need to be updated to include mobile and handheld use – such as no mobiles in changing rooms – and the taking and sharing of electronic images. Such policies are most effective when students are involved in drawing them up and feel a sense of ownership for them – they are then very likely to help ensure that the rules are enforced.

Parents may also need support with home use of mobile devices, particularly if they are part of a school initiative and are either on loan, or families have been required to purchase them. There already exists in schools a lot of good practice around supporting families with safeguarding children online. When tablets are introduced, this can be built on by schools holding open evenings and providing online references and printed materials that outline simple rules and checks for home use. One way to ensure the message gets out is to require that parents take part in training sessions before collecting the devices in person.

Evaluation – keep using the tablets?

Investing in handheld and mobile technologies can be expensive, even if in the short term you have only bought one or two machines to try out. Just as when personal computers first appeared in schools in the early 1980s and are now an integral part of almost every classroom, so tablets and touchscreens are only likely to increase in number. With that in mind you need to know that your investment is bearing fruit, and just what you are getting for your money.

What to evaluate

There are two aspects to critically examining highly portable devices in schools. One is the technology itself; the other is the impact it has, because while these are connected they are not necessarily interdependent. You might provide the device but find it hasn't changed working practices, or teaching and learning in the school. Or you might discover that pupils are producing higher-quality work despite using machines that are proving slow and unreliable.

Are the machines up to scratch?

Even though there will have been a degree of research prior to procuring any machines, there is nothing like owning one to find out if it meets the requirements of your school. Many of these will be practical, such as whether the battery has the stamina to get through the day, or if they are simply too heavy for many students. Others will focus on reliability and robustness, and how quickly they can be turned around if they crash and need attention from the technical support team.

Some of this data is easy enough to compile. Usage will determine if the battery is good enough, and logs of support calls will inform judgements about reliability. Response times will test warranty obligations or managed service commitments from suppliers. Other aspects, such as usability, can be assessed from user feedback, as can their accessibility for users with special needs and disabilities. Having them in your hands will also give a proper sense of how easy they are to use, if they can be held and operated easily, whether the screen is responsive, the cameras sufficiently sharp, and if practical, management considerations such as printing and file sharing can be dealt with well enough.

This evaluation is unlikely to be a one-off, as the pace of change means that new and improved devices will be entering the market frequently. So just because a particular machine meets your current requirements doesn't mean that there isn't a better one coming soon, or that your needs will change – a longer school day perhaps. There may also be issues that don't appear for some time, such as all the batteries failing just after the one-year warranty runs out.

Impact on the school

There can be many reasons for investing in handheld and mobile technologies. It could be to improve processes across the school; to make administrative tasks easier for staff, such as registration or behaviour recording; to cut down the cost of photocopying; or to make a shift from textbooks to ebooks. Or it could be a belief that technology can raise achievement and tablets represent a significant opportunity to bring it into greater and more effective use. And it could be all of these and more.

Whatever the initial reasons, it is against those that evaluation needs to happen. Even an open-ended question, such as, 'What can we do with these devices?' will have an answer that should be recorded. More developed questions might be, 'Can tablets improve maths levels for Year 9?' 'Will regular use of a portable touchscreen improve fine-motor coordination for a dyspraxic pupil?' 'Can using iPads raise the standard of student composition in music?' 'Does immediate reporting of rewards and sanctions in the behaviour monitoring system through the use of handhelds make it more effective?'

Some questions will have easier answers than others. If the bills for photocopying and printer ink fall, then it is probably fair to say that one impact is that staff are providing more electronic resources for students. However, a decrease in lesson absences might be because lessons have become more engaging, or that absences are more quickly reported through electronic registration, or perhaps a combination of both.

There are many ways of structuring an evaluation, all of which involve a process of articulating the reasons for the initiative, determining how any developments might be measured, implementing the change and assessing the impact.

The Education Endowment Foundation[16] has a very useful booklet called *The DIY Evaluation Guide* that outlines the process in more depth. It suggests there are eight steps to the process of determining the impact of any innovations, which can be split into three stages.

Stage 1: Preparation

At this point you need to frame the question, or questions, that you want to answer. It helps to refine these so that there is no ambiguity. If there is a large deployment of devices, then different members of staff may be exploring a range of questions. In order to address these there need to be agreed measures to see what difference the introduction of the technology makes. These will depend on the questions asked, but could be found from attainment data, or surveys of users, or changes in behaviour measured by senior managers being called to remove pupils from lessons.

Strictly speaking there should also be a control group, one that isn't involved in the initiative, so any factors other than the devices can be cancelled out. This can be difficult to do in a school, but comparisons can be made in other ways. For instance, using a group in a previous year who had comparable profiles to the students in the evaluation, or even finding a group in another school following the same scheme of work. Similarly, it is possible to do comparisons over time, working with one group and then another to see whether any impact is repeated.

Even though the results may be imperfect, critically evaluating your implementation will have benefits.

Stage 2: Implementation

As the implementation begins, a benchmark should be made, perhaps a pretest of pupil capabilities, a sample of work or a snapshot of monitoring data. This can then be repeated following the introduction of the machines as a means of establishing the degree of change that has occurred.

The introduction will need to be managed so that either all pupils are assessed and use the devices at the same point and for the same period, or staggered but with a replicated timeframe.

Stage 3: Analysis and reporting

Once the data is in, it needs to be critically examined and any impact recorded and reported. There are a number of audiences for this material. As well as colleagues, pupils and their parents, other schools may well be interested in your results, as will be organisations such as Ofsted.[17] Internally, governors will want to know what benefit has come from the potentially heavy investment in technology.

By sharing the results of their research, schools can support each other in successfully introducing new technologies, and in reaping the rewards in changed practice in teaching and learning, and improved outcomes for learners.

Conclusion

Getting started with highly mobile devices in school isn't necessarily straightforward. The more time and effort you put into research and consideration of what the school's – and more especially the learner's – needs are, the greater the benefits you will accrue.

There is plenty to think about, what with battery life, management, sustainability, training, funding, security, home/school use, insurance and technical support, let alone the apps and resources to use on the device. But the most fundamental question is: 'How will you use them in teaching and learning?' By resolving that question you will more easily be able to focus on what the best technological answer is. And if the answer is 'I don't know,' or 'I'm not sure,' it might be best to pause and reassess. Sure, tablets have their uses in schools, but rushing into getting some without thinking through just what to do with them may mean you struggle to get the best out of them and don't follow through on the investment. Better to resist until you are clear about what they offer than rush to acquire them and struggle to work out what they are for.

Notes

1 The Communication Market 2013 (August): http://stakeholders.ofcom.org.uk/ market-data-research/market-data/communications-market-reports/cmr13/?a=0 (accessed 14 July 2014).

2 Naace (http://www.naace.co.uk/) is a national ICT association made up of educators, technologists and policy makers who wish to advance both teaching and learning through the use of technology.

3 EdFutures (http://edfutures.net/) is a website dedicated to supporting change of the current education system, with a focus on the role that technology might play as a leader for change (or Trojan mouse). It is run by Professor Peter Twining, a senior lecturer at the Open University.

4 The e-Learning Foundation (http://www.e-learningfoundation.com/), which launched in 2001, works in partnership with schools, parents, charities and businesses to provide computers, educational software and internet access to all schoolchildren, especially those from disadvantaged backgrounds and with special learning needs.

5 Tablets for Schools (www.tabletsforschools.co.uk) is a campaigning organisation that regularly conducts independent research around the use of tablet computers in school. Launched in 2012, it is supported by headteachers, schools, leading academics, charities,

industry and Government. Supporters and partners include a number of household names in the technology field, including Google, Sony, Samsung, Microsoft and ICT associations Naace and the e-Learning Foundation.

6 Which? (also known as the Consumers' Association) was set up in 1957 and is well known for its product testing and consumer campaigning. The UK-based independent charity, which includes a magazine and website (www.which.co.uk), is funded solely by subscriptions to support its advocacy campaigns and consumer protection work. It prides itself on not accepting 'advertising, freebies or government funding'. See www.which.co.uk/tabletsize (accessed 14 July 2014).

7 Techradar (www.techradar.com), one of five websites owned by Future, an award-winning media group. This website carries reviews and news features on the latest technology products, including home entertaining and mobile phones (cell phones).

8 The *TES* is a weekly magazine aimed at teachers and further education lecturers and was first published in the UK in 1910. The publication has changed ownership several times since 2005, and is currently owned by TPG Capital LLP, a global private investment firm. *TES* has a readership of more than 350,000 and includes a website (www.tes.co.uk) with more than 2.7 million registered users.

9 MJO Online/Agent4Change.net (www.agent4change.net) is a UK-based online source of information on technology for learning aimed at education professionals. It provides high-quality original news, features, analysis and reviews from a range of contributors and commentators, and is an independent title not affiliated to a trade or professional body.

10 Building Schools for the Future (BSF) was an ambitious £55 billion secondary school rebuilding and renovation programme in England, put in place by the Blair Government. It was overseen by Partnership for Schools, a non-departmental joint venture between the Department for Children, Schools and Families (now the Department for Education), Partnerships UK and private-sector partners. BSF was controversially axed in 2010 by the incoming Education Secretary, Michael Gove, with the explanation that 'it was wasteful and bureaucratic'.

11 The Pupil Premium is additional funding given to schools to support disadvantaged pupils (those eligible for free school meals) and close the attainment gap between them and their peers. It was introduced in 2011 and equates to £900 per child (total for 2013–14 was £1.875 billion). The funding is paid directly, with schools deciding how to use the money.

12 A dongle is a small device that can be plugged into a computer or laptop to give access to the internet wherever there is mobile coverage. Owners pay for the dongle and a fee for monthly or pre-pay internet access.

13 Dropbox – a file-hosting service run by Dropbox Inc, a California-based company. Files placed in this folder can be accessed from any computer or mobile phone.

14 Quick response (QR) codes are similar to bar codes, but capable of holding a lot more information. They have been around since 1994 (initially designed for the Japanese automotive industry) and are simply text that has been encoded in a two-dimensional format that can be read by devices such as a camera or a smartphone. With the growth of smartphone usage, QR codes are increasingly used in advertising campaigns.

15 Google Docs is a freeware web-based office suite offered by Google within its Google Drive service. It allows users to create and edit documents online while collaborating with other users live.

16 Education Endowment Foundation (http://educationendowmentfoundation.org.uk) is a grant-making charity founded in 2011 with a £125 million grant from the Department for Education. It is run by two other trusts – Sutton and Impetus – and aims to support organisations and projects that work to raise the attainment of disadvantaged children.

17 The Office for Standards in Education, Children's Services and Skills (Ofsted) (http://www.ofsted.gov.uk/) is a non-ministerial watchdog responsible for regulating and carrying out regular inspections of state schools, colleges, child minding and daycare in England. Since 2007 Ofsted has also provided inspection for social care services for children and the welfare inspection of independent and maintained boarding schools.

2

Tablets and special educational needs

Great news for children with cognitive difficulties.

Handheld and mobile technologies are causing a stir in classrooms across the country as teachers and learners discover the opportunities that they bring. Nowhere is this excitement more palpable than among educators who work with children and young people with special educational needs. Whether in mainstream or primary schools, across all ages and a diverse range of learning difficulties, this technology is making a difference, especially tablets, and particularly the device that first gave them wide popular appeal, the Apple iPad.

They are a 'disruptive technology' said Martin Littler, chief executive of Inclusive Technology, one of the leading supply companies for specialist ICT resources in the UK. 'iPads are making us think about all aspects of assistive technology (AT) and are bringing change at an amazing, or alarming, rate,' he added, describing them as 'a force of nature and great news for children with cognitive difficulties.'

Despite the excitement, there is need for caution, as there is a danger that iPads are becoming seen as 'the silver bullet that will sort everything out', according to Sally Paveley, ICT teacher at the Bridge School in Islington. While enthused by the possibilities offered by iPads, she said, 'Sometimes people can be over-optimistic.' Despite the warnings she remains a fan though, adding, 'Because they work. Because they are easy to use. Because they can be used up close and personal. The front end is wonderful. It's simple. It's intuitive. It's in your face. Most people can make something happen with it.'

Tablets are a technology with a lot of social cachet, too – 'aspirational and engaging', explained Ben Annett, ICT coordinator at Riverside, a special school in Haringey. 'Kids will see their parents, brothers and sisters using them and want one themselves,' he said, unlike some of the devices aimed at these particular learners. It isn't a 'big, yellow, ugly box with "special needs" stamped all over it'. This is 'cool' technology that doesn't mark the user out as someone who is any different from his or her peers. Martin Littler emphasised, 'The effect is so strong that those with a disability will choose a tablet even if it does not work as well as a dedicated AT device.'

This narrowing of choice might be surprising given the breadth of users' needs and the range of technology available to them on the market. 'There are currently over 150 dedicated communication devices, and at least 40 different vocabulary sets – so there is considerable choice available to meet a very wide range of needs,' pointed out Anna Reeves, centre manager of ACE Centre North, a specialist service for people needing technology to aid their communication. Even though such machines can provide access to a wide variety of software applications, users are choosing the generic device, that might not meet all their communication needs, over the specialist one.

'They offer more intuitive multifunctionality in one device than most dedicated devices,' she explained. 'They are relatively inexpensive, inclusive, multifunctional, motivating, beautiful and cool.' Although she added the caveat that the purchase decision might not always rest with the user: 'There is a risk that the tablet device is often purchased as it is within the comfort – or interest – zone of the purchaser rather than because it's the most appropriate solution to meet the needs of the user.'

Although there are reasons to approach tablets with caution, there are many more to grasp them eagerly and get stuck in. Principally that they are highly portable, with myriad uses and thousands of apps available to do everything you want, and many things you don't.

Their weight, size and battery life mean that they can be taken anywhere and placed just where a child might need one, easily mounted and encased in heavy protection if necessary. At the Bridge School, Sally Paveley explained, 'Lots of children are not comfortable sitting at a conventional workstation, or a laptop on a table, but they would make use of technology if we can bring it to them.

'They [iPads] are very touch-sensitive. You don't need to do an awful lot to make something happen. They are very accessible for our students who are able to use some part of their body to touch them.' Ben Annett agreed, as 'you can get to kids who can't physically engage with other devices' and then 'take it to their hand, or their arm, or whatever they are able to use'.

Positioning is not only important for those with physical impairments; other students may need a device placed in a particular way in order to be able to see it. As Richard Hirstwood, a leading trainer in how to use technology with children with special educational needs explained, 'When we are working with children or students who are visually impaired or have cortical visual impairments, the screen may need to be off to the side, underneath or over the top of somebody's head. Interactive whiteboards, plasma screens and computers in general, are pretty fixed. The tablet isn't.'

Then there are built-in access features, such as text-to-speech and easy screen manipulation through swipes and gestures, along with built-in drivers to specialist devices such as switches (buttons that when pressed bring a response from a connected device or a computer screen) or Braillers. The interface is intuitive, controlled by our instrument of choice for exploration and manipulation – our fingers.

For many children and young people with more complex special needs, such as profound and multiple learning difficulties (PMLD), this brings a greater immediacy than other means of interacting with technology, like switches. As Ben Annett put it, 'There is no distance between the finger and the effect.'

While this ease of use is a benefit, it can also lead to problems as learners can inadvertently – or deliberately – cause unwanted actions in apps, or even leave them altogether. However, features can be locked down to prevent this. 'The thing that has got me stuck with iPads, that has convinced me about them, is the guided access settings,' said Ben Annett, 'Without that you can't guide what the kids are doing.'

It's not just that these are devices that address many of the problems of learners being able to use technology, it's also about what they do with it once they have it. Stephen Drewitt is a research assistant at the Bridge School and he helps staff investigate the most effective ways to use tablets. 'Ease of use is a big thing for our guys,' he said, 'but after that comes motivation. From the cause–and–effect apps used by the PMLD guys up to maths games and stuff like that, what really sets it aside from traditional materials is that it makes all those things more engaging and more fun.'

When Sally Paveley began working with iPads at school it was this aspect of the use of technology – its ability to engage – that she found most promising for some of her students: 'My focus from the beginning was those guys who have very, very extreme sensory needs. Those students who are locked into their own, usually autistic, worlds. Those who find it quite hard to make a communication breakthrough.' For this group it wasn't whether they could physically engage with the device that was the issue, but whether they wanted to.

'You can interact with students with an iPad without them being able to touch it,' she explained, going on to say that the most important thing was 'the interaction you can have with the students using the iPad as a focus'. The flexibility of the device creates all sorts of possibilities, such as 'sitting with somebody and using the camera and pointing it at each other', or 'playing with an app and monitoring somebody's responses – looking for a signal that they want you to do more of it for them'. It is this engagement with the student that can be the point of the session, that 'you are doing something together. You are intervening. They are beginning to tolerate your presence.'

It is not just interactions between teachers and learners that this technology has helped to encourage, it is giving students reasons to talk to each other too. In unstructured sessions Sally Paveley found that they began to show each other the apps they were using, or sharing the websites they were on. This unexpected benefit was quickly spotted by staff and now sixth-form students at the Bridge spend time every Wednesday morning using iPads to get conversations flowing to develop their social skills as part of their preparation for postschool living.

The engaging and absorbing nature of technology can be both a bonus and a source of problems. Many learners, in particular those on the autistic spectrum, are drawn to technology because of its distinctive characteristics, like the fact that it is predictable and follows rules; that the learner can be in control of the interaction; that even if it does something unexpected, control can be regained, even by turning the device off and on again. 'For somebody on the spectrum, technology is an easier place to be than dealing with other human beings, who are horribly unpredictable and scary,' she said.

However, the attractiveness of technology can also present a problem, particularly if its use is not well managed, as Richard Hirstwood explained: 'It is very easy for a tablet to be used as a babysitting device and many children or students who have autism can very easily become obsessive about a particular app.'

The problem can be distinguishing between when learners are using a device as a means of keeping them occupied, to make the adults' lives easier, or as an essential way to help them manage and regulate their emotions. Sally Paveley understood the student's situation as, 'My obsession is helping me to cope with the demands that are being made on me by giving me a feeling of being in control of something.'

If students are in a state of distress they are not in a position to learn: thinking and processing skills are impaired, adrenaline is flowing and 'you are not going to be receptive to being stretched because you are already stretched beyond your limit'; all available energy is going into dealing with the high anxiety they are experiencing. In this instance understanding whether the technology is helping the student to cope or giving the teacher a break is part of a continuum. Recognising the difference and helping the student move on to learning once a sufficiently relaxed state is achieved is part of the 'art and craft of being a teacher or a therapist', Sally explained, although 'for some students it may take a very long time'.

Students' individual use of the iPad can be less of a priority at other times, too. While the accessibility of tablets – their capacity to be used by people with restricted movement or limited cognitive understanding – is one of their attractions, focusing on just this aspect of them limits their usefulness. If the emphasis is placed on students' capacity to use the device for themselves, to be independent users, 'you miss out on a whole lot of learning that isn't about that,' said Sally Paveley. That's because when you highlight cause and effect – getting a student to touch the screen to produce a response – then staff tend to step back because 'they think they have succeeded if the student can do a bit of prodding and make something happen. It really needs to be a much fuller experience than that.'

Richard Hirstwood agreed: 'Simply letting children and students occupy themselves on iPads is akin to a group sat around watching a DVD. It may be great fun. It may be useful. But what's really happening?' A child using a tablet is not necessarily in itself a fruitful educational experience.

'Tablets need to be treated in the same way as we would a book; we need to create a multisensory experience around the app we are using,' he added. 'Touchy-feely things and nasty smells still need to be used alongside these new devices.'

There are, then, aspects of teaching and learning in special schools that tablets are particularly adept at supporting, but they can also have an impact on the established curriculum. In ICT lessons Sally Paveley has been teaching students for some years about taking digital photographs: iPads have transformed these lessons.

Previously a lot of time was spent on learning how to use digital cameras, which could prove a challenge, particularly with the need for accuracy in framing the image in the viewfinder, conceptual understanding of what the outcome would look like and having the necessary motor control to trigger the shutter. Using tablets resolved these issues in five minutes, rather than several weeks, and the focus shifted to one of communication, getting students to take portrait photos, entailing giving and receiving instructions, then talking about the outcomes and critically evaluating them. 'It meant we were able to look at the higher-order skills of photography rather than simply the mechanics of how you take a photograph,' she explained, 'In the past we only got as far as taking something that wasn't blurred or wasn't upside down.'

Use of the camera is something that Ben Annett finds very helpful in lessons, although for different purposes. The simplicity of recording and playback means that teachers can capture lesson content and straight away play it back, in PE for instance, or when rehearsing social skills, learning British Sign Language or practising a presentation. 'There is a real immediacy,' he said. 'You can video something, then view it immediately.'

The range of tools and resources available on tablets gives rise to a host of possibilities for ways of working. They are very open-ended. As Sally Paveley put it, 'It's a bit like a pencil. It makes marks. What can you do with it?' Or as Richard Hirstwood suggested, 'There are lots of limitations, but it's not really to do with the devices themselves, it's the way we use them.'

Where negatives arise it is usually around technical and management issues. Anna Reeves found that, 'The hardware has not been developed for AAC [augmentative and alternative communication], therefore issues such as speaker volume and mounting opportunities have not necessarily been developed at the design stage.' And Martin Littler conceded that the possibilities of tablets are 'still well short of what can be achieved with dedicated VOCA [voice output communication aid] devices'.

As for looking after them in a school environment, many of the problems are at a level removed from most of the staff. 'The whole multiuser thing is a conundrum,' explained Ben Annett. 'They are personal devices with no way to offload work on to a network. They are very locked down.' While Sally Paveley reported that the ICT manager at the Bridge is on 'a very steep learning curve'.

However, it seems that tablets are having such a positive impact in classrooms that technical difficulties are outweighed and forgiven. But is this situation unique to the iPad, or is this a bubble ready to burst? 'I haven't come across one that works quite as nicely as the iPad yet,' said Sally Paveley, explaining their popularity. Although Richard Hirstwood took a more pragmatic view: 'There is no question that at the moment iOS is ahead of Android in education in the UK. However, in the future the operating system will become less important. Many non-technical people really can't tell much difference between iOS and Android.'

Perhaps the distinction is artificial. That what we really need to do is recognise and celebrate the paradigm shift that these devices represent and look forward to the exciting possibilities that they herald. As Martin Littler put it, 'With iPads and other tablets we have the beginnings of the dream device from the standpoint of accessibility and inclusion. Why would any learner with cognitive difficulties want to be "wired up" to a PC when everything they could want to do is so easily accessed on such a cool device?'

The practice

3

The Flitch Green Academy

Confidence is a crucial component of success.

Challenge is very much part of the curriculum at Flitch Green Academy in Dunmow, Essex,[1] so much so that it is on the timetable. Half an hour a day is given over to children taking on a range of tasks focused on developing five key life skills which are integral to the curriculum and achieved through taking on various projects over an extended period, usually a couple of weeks.

These life skills – critical thinker, cool collaborator, challenge conqueror, creative navigator and confident character – are displayed around the school, along with Mr Trogon, the school's own cartoon bird that embodies the skills and encourages the children. The pupils help to formulate the projects, and are asked to review how well they think they have done in meeting the challenge and the key skills it has helped to develop. Previous examples of challenges have included creating a dinosaur museum, putting on a mystery evening, recording a poetic river podcast and making a superhero animation.

School principal Nathan Lowe explains:

> The teachers gather the children's ideas together: What do they know? What do they want to know? And then the teachers take them away and match them up to the curriculum that they need to deliver. So the children feel they are driving their own learning, which I guess, in a way they are.

The impact of the focus on these skills is tangible. An air of calm confidence permeates the school, in both the children and the staff at every level. They are prepared to take risks, rise to challenges and trust in the skills and capabilities of everyone in creating a thriving learning community. As it says in the school prospectus, 'Confidence is a crucial component of success.'

While technology is seen as fundamental to learning at Flitch Green, it is not fêted as the answer to educationists' prayers; it is just another tool in the box. As Nathan Lowe puts it, 'My belief is that it is about the right tool for the right job. That might be a pencil, paintbrush or paper; it may be a MacBook or iPad. You often go into lessons and you often see some children on the floor with iPads, some in their books, some on the MacBook.' The role the technology plays is to help motivate and enrich learning, to involve and engage children in their curriculum.

The school opened five years ago with 55 pupils, and 100 MacBook laptops. Since then it has invested in iPods and, more recently after a successful trial, 80 iPads – ten in each of the eight classrooms. As an establishment it is always interested in the latest technologies, not for their own sake but for how they can enhance learning.

During a recent open evening children and parents followed a trail around the school using quick response (QR) codes to solve puzzles, and get the next clue (like barcodes, QR codes are 'swiped' by the mobile devices to reveal more information). Chromakey or 'green-screen' technology is used fairly regularly for all sorts of activities. Normally a green or blue backdrop is used for filming – and that colour background can then be removed in production and superimposed with an alternative background. It is the technique they use for weather forecasts on TV and that is why it is such a popular feature in schools.

Nathan Lowe believes that having a range of technologies available increases the options within the classroom. 'It gets teachers thinking about the learning. It's focusing the teachers on what they want the children to learn and how this technology is going to enable that. There are times when it won't. There are times when your maths book, your English book and your pencil and paper will, but it's giving teachers an extra tool.' Beyond that, he also acknowledges that technology can be a particular draw for children: 'It's up to us as 21st-century educators to harness what they are interested in and use that to our best advantage.'

Around the school there are plenty of examples of this philosophy in evidence. Reception children have been making their own cookery programme demonstrating recipes for different sorts of soup. They have taken turns to describe the ingredients and the process, using green-screen technology to provide appropriate scenarios such as a TV studio kitchen.

'You will need a tomato from the garden,' the first child on screen says, in front of an image of tomato plants growing. 'Pour in water and get the herbs,' says the next pupil in the film, as the scenario changes to show her in a kitchen with a measuring jug. The final version, edited with the help of some of the children, will be posted on the class blog for parents to see. All the classes have them, and they are set up to receive comments like responses from parents. Comments are moderated before being posted.

The videos will be available on the class iPads for the children to watch. Information and stills from them will be used in wall displays.

'Higher up the school,' says Nathan Lowe, 'one of the Year 4 classes was doing "The *Titanic* Experience", looking at what happened to the *Titanic*[2] and focusing on weather and weather forecasts.' The pupils working in groups were tasked with creating their own weather forecasts for different areas of the world to see how they varied. 'They had to research the weather in different countries. They filmed it on an iPad, put it into iMovie on a MacBook, edited it, added some music, and that is going to be posted on their class blog.'

The children are very comfortable with the technology available to them, and perfectly at ease when talking about what it does and what they have done with it. 'Story Kit,' says Charlie from Year 2, pointing to one of the apps on the iPad on the table in front of him, happy to show off what he knows. Rory, his classmate, echoes him, 'Story Kit'. Charlie mentions 'Sketch' before Rory goes on to explain that the device can 'make photos'. They both then settle on showing off Puppet Pals.

With a gentle prompt they move from the apps to show what they have done with them. 'In Venus class we used it learning about the Victorians,' explains Rory, 'We had loads of pictures and . . . ' 'You chose some,' Charlie cuts in helpfully.

With a bit of searching they found animations they had made of a peach being blown out of a volcano, complete with narrative over the top. It was work based on the class book, *James and the Giant Peach*.

Their schoolmates in Year 4 have been working on the human body, having to explain the roles of the different parts. 'Writing paragraphs about the lungs, skeleton, heart and muscles,' Aryan says, outlining the task. They started with finding information on Wikipedia, then used this to make a brochure in Pages. 'I got some pictures and then I got some captions,' explained Aryan.

His classmate Emily chose a different app, Book Creator, to create her ebook about muscles. 'I got some facts here,' she says, showing a page that says there are 650 muscles. 'It takes 45 just to smile.' She has provided more information with a diagram of how muscles work, and then a video that she has embedded in the book.

As the iPads are shared in the class, Emily also shows off her friend Alisha's response to the task. Using the device's integral video camera she has made a short film explaining how muscles work, while flexing her arm and talking about what is happening. Matter-of-factly she adds, 'I did a Keynote presentation on the heart.'

Aryan adds that his class used 123D Sculpt in science to design different soles on shoes to get the best grip on ice, and in maths to explore shape symmetry, before Charlie chips in that he can use iMovie, and that in Photo Booth you can choose from 'different effects'.

The enthusiasm for learning, along with the confidence to talk about it, and the opportunities the technology provides are clear. So what's the impact in the classroom?

Nathan Lowe believes, 'We are going away from the position of having one knowledgeable person in the room lecturing to the children. Now it's about us all learning together. The teacher is almost a facilitator.' The way the children are choosing to demonstrate what they have learnt is also significant. He described them as 'content creators rather than content consumers – sharing their learning in different ways'. And the impact on the learners? 'I think it has made them more confident, able and independent – comfortable with taking risks and prepared for the challenge when learning new things.'

But the impact on staff is more mixed, he says. As with the children, they have more to think about, although the impact of that has varied. 'We've got different groups of teachers,' he explains. 'We've got the ones who have been here from the very start and they have been on that journey. It has developed their knowledge and their understanding of that teaching and learning process more. They are much more confident and capable of using technology.'

It is a process that he is quick to admit he has found challenging during his own time at the school. Now, as principal, he is responsible for bringing in new staff and inducting them into the Flitch Green philosophy of teaching and learning, and the use of technology to support this.

With the important role of technology in the school, is ICT competence part of the selection criteria? 'It is certainly not something they have to have, but it is certainly desirable,' he says. But what is more important is 'getting that right person – one that has the passion and wants to work here'.

It can be a steep learning curve getting new teachers up to speed after a September start, but it's an approach that can sell itself: 'They soon begin to see the benefits of our curriculum and the use of technology.'

It is the positive effect on pupils' learning that Nathan Lowe sees as the most persuasive argument for investing time, energy and money in new technologies. He believes that once staff appreciate its impact on outcomes they are prepared to adopt it themselves.

> It's about showing teachers the benefit. What they are going to get out of using some of this kit in their classrooms. How it is going to make their lives easier. How it will give improved outcomes for children. When you get a small group of keen people on board you can let them spread that good practice around.

It's this shared ownership of new ways of working and the responsibility for their adoption that he sees as key to success. The senior leadership team may suggest ideas, but it is the staff who are responsible for their implementation and development.

> It is very much the teachers. They are quite a creative bunch. They come up with a lot of ideas that are bounced around in the classroom that change and become even bigger. The leadership team guides things in the right direction but also teachers, teaching assistants and the children are very much part of it, driving and directing things.

Such positive attitudes are also exhibited by other members of the school community. 'The parents are excited by it,' explains Nathan Lowe. 'They want to send their children here. They love what we do.' To a large extent, this is because of the children going home enthused about their learning and wanting to talk about it.

However, he's aware that some people misunderstand the role of technology. 'I still think that, from the outside looking in, some still think all the children do is sit and play on their iPads all day.' The way to counter such perceptions is to engage with them and make sure parents are thoroughly informed:

> We are having some curriculum sessions with parents to talk them through what we do, to let them know how we are using our iPads as a tool. It is when

they actually look a bit further into it and see our curriculum that they then realise it is the learning that is at the heart of everything. The technology is just the tool to deliver it really.

The use of technology in class is also a reflection of what is happening in the wider world. As he puts it, 'This is the world that the children are growing up in. If they don't use the technology in school, they will go home and use it.'

This availability of technology at home has enabled the school to make more use of different channels to connect with them electronically. 'I think it makes communication with parents and the outside world much easier,' says Nathan Lowe. 'We create weekly newsletters. The class blogs are updated regularly.' With more frequent information becoming available to parents, 'it has taken away a lot of the niggles and the little questions'.

It is not simply communication with parents that technology has opened up. Educators from across the world are getting in touch, and sometimes turning up in person too. 'A teacher from New Zealand contacted us,' he recalls. 'She had a month-long trip to Europe. She came and spent the day with us. Last year we linked up with her school. My class created some profiles about themselves and, using Dropbox, we sent them to her. Just seeing the children's faces when they realised their work has been viewed on the other side of the world brings home the fact that this is a powerful tool.'

In 2012, before he became the principal, Nathan Lowe's class was already exploring global links in lessons. 'I set my class blog up and I put the map on there so you could see where people were coming from. You had all sorts of countries. When the children could see their work was being seen by people from across the globe it really motivated and inspired them.'

Flitch Green has many connections – locally, nationally and internationally – and it wants to help other schools to work in a similar way. The school has enjoyed and benefited from close links with another forward-thinking, innovative school, Essa Academy[3] in Bolton (see Chapter 6), and Nathan Lowe believes his school should follow Essa's lead. 'I don't think we share enough good practice with other schools,' he says, despite reeling off a number of local links, including 'Felsted School down the road and a couple of schools in Braintree'.

With the strong emphasis on the use of technology across the curriculum, there is less need for a formal ICT curriculum, although this increased access arguably makes for a greater need to ensure pupils are well equipped to look after themselves online. Esafety is not forgotten but, rather like learning about ICT itself, it is a constant theme. As Nathan Lowe puts it, 'We need to make sure it is drip-fed into our curriculum.'

One other issue that the school needs to confront is replacing equipment as it wears out, having been so richly endowed when it opened its doors in 2008. Most of the devices are of the same age and it's beginning to show. 'That's our worry,' he concedes, 'that they will all go at once. We are aware that we are going to need to start refreshing some of them.'

Having branched out into different types of technology, developing a mixed economy of devices, and always being prepared for flexibility and innovation could mean that there may be no single option for replacement. As with everything else, the school will be comfortable with that challenge, learning from it and finding the positives.

Reflecting on Flitch Green's success so far, Nathan Lowe concludes: 'It's not just because of the technology. I think it is down to the staff we've got here and the culture and the climate we've created. With the use of the technology it all comes together as a package.'

Notes

1 Flitch Green, Dunmow, Essex, UK: http://theflitchgreenacademy.co.uk/ (accessed 14 July 2014).
2 *RMS Titanic* was, in its time, the largest passenger ship in the world. It sank in the North Atlantic on its maiden voyage in 1912, killing 1,490 people (www.rmstitanic.net/).
3 Essa Academy, a secondary school in Bolton, was one of the first UK schools to implement 1:1 mobile technology (www.essaacademy.org/).

4

Normanby Primary School

Children are only in lessons for five hours a day so why not give them simple tools to help grasp learning opportunities at other times and in other places?

There's an open-door policy for learning at Normanby Primary School[1] – in all senses.

Lessons are taking place as usual in the classrooms leading off a corridor that is almost square and substantial in size. All their doors are open, so the teachers have clear sight of the groups of children milling around the corridor.

Aged between nine and ten, they are engrossed in their tasks, taking it in turns to use their iPod Touch to film each other's presentation about Greek food – part of a larger class project on the ancient Greeks. As they work the air is filled with verbal clues: 'green screen', 'feedback', 'import' and 'upload'.

After editing and re-editing the video recordings made on them, the children add their own original images (and some downloaded ones) and then email their polished products to their class teacher to be shared and discussed with the rest of the class for instant response. This lively activity contributes to the infectious energy that permeates Normanby school and is an eye-popping reminder of how fully the pupils and teachers have integrated handheld, mobile technology into everyday learning and teaching.

Getting to the stage where, for the past four years, every child entering Year 5 at the Middlesbrough primary school for 3–11-year-olds is given an iPod Touch to use at home and in school has been no mean feat. Headteacher since 2008, Carl Faulkner says his 'light bulb' moment came back in the days of simple Palm devices. He used one as a diary and to take notes.

'I realised I could carry around my working life in that handheld device and access it at a time and place that suited me,' he says. 'Children are only in lessons for five hours a day so why not give them simple tools to help grasp learning opportunities at other times and in other places.' He was sure handheld devices would directly support independent learning as well as encourage collaboration across the whole school community, especially between home and school.

The opportunity to test his theory came when the school decided to review its curriculum. Soon discussions among staff and students focused on the value of mobile technologies for learning and whether their integration would remove some of the barriers to learning which, Carl Faulkner concedes, 'we sometimes set up ourselves in school'.

> You could talk for hours about how the devices let you do new things, but I can't get my head around it being something new. I want a classroom where the children are engaged, talking to each other, collaborating to do things.

> We were doing that – with the worksheets, setting problems and challenges in the class – before the devices came along and we are doing it now that they are here because that's how we want our curriculum to be at our school. But what is different, in particular with the iPods, is that it makes the engagement and collaboration happen all the time and the technology is reliable.

Carl Faulkner doesn't go along with the laissez-faire notion that it doesn't matter which devices children and teachers use. It does. They have to be absolutely fit for purpose so they don't get in the way of the learning.

> It is all about having something that teachers can readily adapt to the way they teach and the way that children learn best. So it's not the new things that they do, it's that they let you do the stuff you know you want to do anyway, really well. The devices give us a level playing field and give different children within that the chance to shine.

Looking around at his colleagues, he continues, 'We could all probably think of children over the years that have shone when they are given a handheld device that's theirs to cherish, to take care of. That maybe wouldn't have happened in a traditional classroom.'

Initially, Windows devices were the technology of choice for Normanby, and they are still used around the school. So too are iPads, but, according to Carl Faulkner, the school's aspirations soon found them wanting. The iPod Touch was always favoured by the children, and the school discovered that it provided all the functions they needed, including photography and video for capturing information, and apps for every curriculum subject and learning stage. The message from Normanby is that the learning guides the purchase of the resources and thus began the school's 1:1 mobile programme.

In the planning process, two things were vital for the school. The first was that the device had to be easy for the children to carry and use at home no matter what the situation. 'I don't want a child lugging a laptop down the street on his or her back. I want it safely tucked away in a pocket,' says Carl Faulkner. 'Not every child has a nice straightforward family life and a small device can be used very flexibly, is instantly turned on, and can be easily charged up to bring in to school next day.'

The second was that, regardless of family income, all 65 children in the last year of the school would have an iPod Touch. Currently they cost around £160 depending on the model. Those parents who are able to pay contribute two-thirds towards the cost and the remainder is met out of the school's budget. For families in difficult circumstances, Carl Faulkner says that he does what headteachers do.

> We juggle money from one pot to another and you come out with something that is equitable and fair to the ones that have paid and to the ones that haven't.

> If you haven't paid, the device isn't yours at the end of Year 6. If you've paid reasonably in the way that we agreed at the start, then it is yours at the end of Year 6. If you don't pay, the children still get to use it in the classroom but it doesn't go home and we offer additional minutes out of lesson time for the children who can't take the device home so they can do the extra things. The harsh reality is if I let 60 devices go home unpaid for, how many would come back on Monday?

Kicking off in the summer term of Year 4, there is a lot of coming to terms with managing the device, the rules covering getting it to school and making sure it is brought in fully charged. The process creates conversations with parents about esafety and helps them apply rules at home that clearly complement what happens in school.

As the device and learners move through Year 5 there is apparently a big impact on speaking and listening skills and the children's desire to be involved in the work and the research. Although the device is less prominent in Year 6 due to exams and 'hoops to jump through', there is still the enthusiasm and willingness to talk. 'But if you look through the literacy books, you'll see edited work,' says Carl Faulkner. 'They have learned the skills digitally that they are happy to replicate using pen and pencil.'

Every learning experience at Normanby is shared. The learners have access to their own Apple ID so they and their parents can take ownership and decide on what extra apps they'd like on the devices, and teachers share work with each other all the time. The result is that children enjoy a consistency of experience across classrooms that they didn't have before. 'It could be construed as a negative by some teachers who are not allowed to exist in their own little classroom bubble, but I think my staff see it as a positive,' says Carl Faulkner.

> You can't be closing your door to your staff, the staff can't close the door to each other. They have to talk to keep the lessons flowing in parallel with each other and I think there is a confidence that spills out if you adapt to the change that this aspect of working with the young people brings. It makes you confident about other things.

And the Normanby community has much to celebrate. Its pioneering work with mobile technology has attracted international attention (visits are frequent) and has earned plaudits.[2] In 2009 the headteacher gained the Primary Practitioner award at Handheld Learning Awards[3] and the school was winner in the primary innovation category for using games machines, PDAs and laptops 'to support learning in school and at home', which is proof, he says, that, 'We are doing something that's worth persevering with.'

> We have had recognition for what we're doing from outside of school, which I think helps governors and parents, in particular, feel reassured in times of change and challenge that it's all right for us to have a Normanby way of doing things.

> Schools have a quite high-stakes judgement culture now – you're judged on your SATS, you're judged on your Ofsted – so we've found other ways of being recognised for what we are doing and that builds self-confidence. I think our approach to teaching and learning has had an impact on SATS results and the technology is part of that, but it's not leading it.

There is no question the initiative supports the school's strategy for assessment. In fact, the question gets an emphatic 'Yes, it absolutely, explicitly does,' from Carl Faulkner.

> The biggest thing that we do is talk frequently about assessment in staff meetings – both summative and formative. We've developed simple systems for the teachers to use for the formative assessment, and probably like most schools, we have some agreed marking scheme. We'll have an agreed set of methods that we teach towards and we've got an agreed curriculum for each year group.

> This is helping to develop the culture where the children are going to collaborate to produce a piece of work that is greater than the sum of its parts, and the quicker you give the feedback in relation to the task, the more appropriate and the more relevant the feedback is going to be. You've only got one adult in the classroom so it's a bit of an epic fail if you make that one adult the source of all the feedback within the classroom.

> You can't enforce a traditional classroom plan on children that are working quicker and harder than you can teach. You can't rein them back in. The kids aren't going to want to stop because they are 'naughty'; it's because they are fired up and they are working. You've just got to go with it, which is fantastic.

One of the key things for successful integration of mobile devices is confidence in the technical backup. Any issues with the iPods are easily dealt with through iTunes and good contingency planning. After all, says Carl Faulkner, you always have a few spare pens and pencils when teaching a lesson on writing, so why wouldn't you do the same things with IT equipment?

He admits there is a general challenge on how to get the everyday information that they all need – children, their parents and teachers – on to the mobile devices.

Should there be a specific 'school app' to do this? Perhaps they could get technical, but in reality what Normanby needs are development partnerships that it just doesn't have – yet. In essence he'd like them to work closely with apps developers in much the same way as educationists works closely with education software developers.

> There is a whole world of apps out there and we've just played with the idea but not got very far at all about being in control of what these apps do or say. As an educationist, I think we should be all over that as an issue.

> We need to work closely with app developers to make sure they serve the children well in future. We need to keep listening to the children. Their voice was powerful in leading us to the iPod Touch, and we must make sure we are always ready to use the best tools available to give children the best learning opportunities they can have.

> My vision is a Normanby school app that has a bit of the learning platform, a bit of our school website, a bit of our paper-based communication, a bit of the planners and a bit of the Facebook and Twitter-style relationship for home–to–school as well.

Although there is plenty of information on the school's website – timetables, a blog featuring children's work and lesson content – that parents can access, it's still something that they have to seek out. 'We want to be pushing stuff out to people,' says Carl Faulkner. 'We want to be selling our message about the behaviour, the celebrations in school, as well as all the curriculum stuff. We want to be forcing that down parents' necks because we are proud of what we are doing.'[4]

For Carl Faulkner what is happening at Normanby is absolutely replicable. Of course equipment gets damaged or broken and systems are in place for dealing with that. Children see their technology just as another pencil in their case. 'It's gone from being the hundred and whatever pounds' worth of pencil in the pencil case to being just another thing,' he says. 'As a leader I have to get that message across to staff that broken screens do matter and we want the kids to take care of things, but it's a lot less financially limiting to us as a school than doing a laptop program.'

Normanby may have made giant strides forward but there is no complacency. There's a recognition that this is the start and there's a lot more to do. Plans are under way to start an ebook loan library system with children able to download any book they want to any device, even those at home – Kindle, smartphone and, of course, the iPod Touch. The idea is the book will stay on the device for two weeks, after which it will automatically return to the virtual shelf.

If iPods were seen to be having a negative effect at any time, he says, there would be no hesitation in dispensing with them and moving on.

> It is important to keep that awareness of what's working in school and keep asking the question so we are ready to go to the next thing straight away, not dithering around.

I used to hate going to the IT suite to switch all the computers on and try and keep the kids quiet for ten minutes only to find out I've forgotten the password and this, that and the other. That's gone. It is a challenge, you've got to learn something different but we've also removed a whole world of hardship and pain from some teachers' lives.

Although iTunes might not yet qualify as an educational content distribution service for the convenience of teachers, Carl Faulkner is more than happy to put what he describes as a 'data Dyson'[5] into the hands of Normanby's eager young learners. 'Combine that with bright, sparky teachers and you are setting up children so that they've got every opportunity to learn.'

Notes

1 Normanby Primary School: www.redcar-cleveland.gov.uk/normanbyprimary (accessed 14 July 2014).
2 For a report about Carl Faulkner's awards for his pioneering work with mobile technology, see *Gazette Live*, 10 May 2010: www.gazettelive.co.uk/news/local-news/normanby-primary-school-headteacher-honoured-3704522 (accessed 14 July 2014).
3 For a report about Carl Faulkner's Handheld Learning Primary Practitioner and Primary Innovation award, see Agent4change.net, 6 October 2009: www.agent4change.net/events/awards/419-teachers-in-the-frame-at-handheld-learning-09-awards.html (accessed 14 July 2014).
4 For links to online courses written by Normanby staff and hosted through iTunes U, see: https://itunes.apple.com/gb/course/normanby-primary-school-foundation/id584760731 (accessed 14 July 2014); https://itunes.apple.com/gb/course/normanby-primary-ibooks/id665806534 (accessed 14 July 2014); https://itunes.apple.com/gb/course/world-war-ii-for-upper-key/id584760128 (accessed 14 July 2014); https://itunes.apple.com/gb/course/pirates/id586897578 (accessed 14 July 2014); https://itunes.apple.com/gb/course/year-6-handbook-guide-for/id584760476 (accessed 14 July 2014); https://itunes.apple.com/gb/course/transport/id586898826 (accessed 14 July 2014); https://itunes.apple.com/gb/course/parent-and-carer-guide-to-y5/id586895739 (accessed 14 July 2014); https://itunes.apple.com/gb/course/ancient-greeks/id586893580 (accessed 14 July 2014).
5 This analogy refers to a piece of equipment that can 'suck up knowledge' as efficiently as a particularly efficient vacuum cleaning device created by British inventor and industrial designer James Dyson.

5

Oakdale Junior School

It's all about the personalisation.

While the arguments about using mobile devices in schools continue to be recycled around them, Dawn Hallybone[1] and her students simply get on with their work and wonder what all the fuss is about. They use Nintendo games consoles just a little bigger than a make-up compact in novel ways in their classroom, and she says this has 'transformed elements of my teaching and the students' learning experience'.

This deputy head and ICT coordinator at Oakdale Junior School[2] in Redbridge, east London, was an early convert to the educational qualities of mobile technology in general and to the Nintendo DS Lite games console in particular, and for her and the pupils, the revolution is not the technology – it is the changing role of the teacher to make the most of the technology and establish mobile learning as a teaching method in its own right.

Four years later, the Nintendo DS Lite is an established teaching tool at Oakdale, used by members of staff, including teaching assistants, and right across the curriculum.

Oakdale is a three-form entry school with around 350 students covering the 7–11 junior age range and they share 30 of the consoles. The dual-screen, handheld game consoles, which most of the children joining the school are already familiar with, come with a touchscreen that is easy to use for writing on and a wireless internet connection. Their work with the Nintendo DS is so much at the heart of the school's curriculum that the timetable for each year group includes using the consoles daily.

Explaining that the plan from the start of the project, which began in 2008, was for the consoles to be used throughout the school, from Year 3 through to Year 6, Dawn Hallybone says they wanted to gauge the effect of the mobile technology on both the teachers and the learners. The driving force would be the impact it would have on learning, particularly if it could change the students' attitude towards mathematics. Consequently, the children use the DS's Brain Training program to do mental maths for short periods, 20 minutes at a time.

The introduction of the devices to Oakdale's classrooms took the learners by surprise. They didn't expect to see the same mobile devices they use for entertainment at home being employed in the classroom. They thought Nintendos could never be part of school, says Dawn Hallybone. 'But now it is normal,' she adds, 'and enables the children to access games and learning at their own speed.'

'The attitude towards mathematics was quite positive before we started using the technology, but children were not always learning their times tables, and we wanted to see if using a different tool would promote this.'

It is a form of learning by stealth, or 'secret learning', according to one of Dawn Hallybone's Year 6 learners. 'They know it's a game, so they don't think it's learning,' she says. 'Straight away they think it's going to be something fun.'

With the aid of the DS Lites pupils are now in control of their own learning, keeping a record of their scores at the back of their books and also their timings, which are then noted by the teacher or teaching assistant. This 'personalisation of learning' has shown a marked increase in competition within the class, according to Dawn Hallybone, which she feels is a good thing. But it is competitiveness with a difference.

'While using the Brain Training program the children are competing against themselves, not with each other,' she explains. 'And they use the other range of titles we use for the DS in the same way.' These include Word Coach, Flip books, Professor Layton, Nintendogs or the PictoChat facility, part of the standard DS package, to explore vocabulary, reading and spelling and to create an in-class chatroom. Each year group now has a set of either DS or 3DS consoles with games such as Pokemon: Typing Adventure and Art Academy for use in class as part of, for example, guided reading.[3]

Mobile technology has helped to create an environment of engagement and encouragement at Oakdale. During lessons children unhesitatingly suggest strategies they could use to work out problems and mental calculation, and discuss questions they might want to put into the machine and why.

In literacy and geography lessons and for cross-curricular review they use Professor Layton,[4] a non-linear puzzle where Professor Layton and his buddy Luke have to follow clues to solve the mystery of the golden apples. Children work in groups on the DS consoles, but also with old-fashioned pen and paper to work on descriptive and instructional writing with the game, with its characters the main drivers. The lesson could include a discussion on how they would use the clues to find the golden apples or they could even produce a newspaper report about the progress of Professor Layton and Luke in their quest.

The variety of activities and learning outcomes are many, including improved hand–eye coordination. Art and design also come into play, with learners creating their own characters for the game.

The formalised measuring of success through monitoring and checking results does have its place, but sometimes it can simply be documented by a change of attitude or behaviour. At Oakdale these changes are in abundance. 'Success in mathematics,' says Dawn Hallybone, 'is where you see children enjoying their maths lessons, engaging more and wanting to go home and learn their tables and as a result, but not for all of them, maths has improved.'

The story for literacy is similar, and while it is accepted that the use of the DS technology in lessons is not the sole driver of the learning improvement, their use is another strategy to support the young learners.

The school ran a short trial using WordCoach software with six children to look at their spelling ages. 'The result was their spelling age from September to January rose eight months,' said Dawn Hallybone, 'with some going up more than a year. This was done in combination with other teaching tools and I worked with them three times a week. They liked the fact that nobody could see if they went horribly wrong and they could go back and re-try for their own benefit. It's all about the personalisation.'

However, there have been what some might consider failures at Oakdale. Not many and none that couldn't be overcome in re-runs with a healthy helping of hindsight. Like remembering to make sure the consoles are kept fully charged with up-to-date reminders in place, and ensuring success by effective forward planning, securing buy-in from everyone involved.

'Sometimes the writing has not been as successful as we'd want, because we've needed to play the game longer,' admits Dawn Hallybone. 'But on the whole, it's all about putting everything into context first. It's not about just giving students the DS so there is quite a lot of planning for teachers. We have learnt as we've trialled the project that you have to see how it fits into your curriculum and what to use it for. We learned that it was important for the key people to go away and use the DS and the games to become confident and then we can trickle that learning down so we kind of cascade the pyramid.'

Four years on, Oakdale believes the initial £2,400 outlay for the 30 consoles was a worthwhile investment, especially considering the number of children who've used them over the years, and continue to use them as a tool for learning. With true creativity, they've built on that initial spend by increasing the collection of games with some freebies – thanks to the writing talent of their learners.

'Sometimes we've been sent games on trial and the children respond by writing reviews about them, saying what they liked or didn't and perhaps how the games could be improved,' she explains. 'To show their appreciation of what they think is valuable feedback, the developers allow them to keep the games. The children loved the exercise because they had a real audience for their writing and they felt that they had earned them for the school.'

That original suite of 30 Nintendo DS Lites at Oakdale has become a rallying point for teachers in other schools in the Redbridge local authority. It gave notice that these machines could be used for powerful learning as well as entertainment.

Now other schools in the borough are using one kind of mobile technology or another, from Nintendo DS to Wiis, notepads and tablets, to enhance teaching and learning. The result has been the formation of the Redbridge Games Network,[5] which has found favour with Dawn Hallybone,[6] who is a strong believer in sharing good practice.

Through the network they share resources, including games and consoles, and also replicate and build on good practice through blogs, photographs and visits to each other's schools. 'We go to conferences to talk about the project and hear from people who say they are replicating our work in a way that suits their own environment,' adds Dawn Hallybone.

> For learners this has been an extra tool that has allowed them to become more engaged and to work at their own pace and in ways that don't tie them to the classroom. It's given them a media outlet and meaning for their writing. Moreover, it's cross-curricular and we can all sit down on the floor with them, and it doesn't matter where we are in the school – we can make use of them to enable and improve communication. A range of strategies and learning outcomes from the one device.

What has it meant for teachers and the wider school community? Parents are pleased about the increased engagement and it has given teachers an extra dimension – it's a different way of teaching and a different way of communicating with the children by talking to them about how they would use the consoles at home and what they like about using them.

> In class you might show them a picture and point out something that's really nice, then ask them to think of a better word than nice. Normally in the classroom, I'd have to wait for 30 hands to go up. As a teacher I can instantly see those responses on the screen of the DS. This improves their vocabulary and we can pick up spellings. It's more immediate than waiting for 30 hands.

From its inception, Oakdale's use of mobile technology has matured to become a permanent fixture in its classrooms. It is so well supported by the school's leadership team and the local authority that it is guaranteed that the digital leaders and at least one teacher in each year group will disseminate the practice. More importantly, it is now also driven by the children.

Although the DS consoles are not connected to the internet, the theme of esafety is a constant at the Oakdale. It is something staff and learners take seriously and cover throughout the year through special assemblies, drop-in sessions led by Dawn Hallybone, as well as on dedicated Internet Safety days.

'One of the best things about the DS [consoles],' explains Dawn Hallybone, 'is that they are so easy to use. We use the children now as guides, so from a management point of view there is a very low skill threshold for teachers to reach. Esafety-wise, they are not connected to the wireless network and pupils know that if we use the PictoChat and message facility, they are not to be inappropriate to each other. In any event they are supervised just as they would be if they were working on another platform.'

By making sure the consoles are securely locked away at the end of each day there have been no major losses apart from four games. But given the small size of the game cartridges, maybe that was inevitable.

Although the project as a whole, and especially Brain Training for maths, has been a big success story for Oakdale, both for mental maths and algebra, Dawn

Hallybone agrees there is a time and place for technology. The school made sure that parents and governors were deeply involved in the decision to bring the consoles into the classrooms. 'We make it very clear with the children that using the Brain Training helps them with their maths. These tools are now familiar to our children and they provide a valuable tool in my arsenal that sits alongside the traditional methods.'

She refutes the suggestion that such methods are seen by some as a poor substitute for traditional teaching. 'We don't sit down and play computer games for three hours a day,' she says. 'We wouldn't read a child a book for three hours. We use games in short, sharp bursts which, if you look at revision programmes, is how you should revise.'

The mobile technology revolution at Oakdale is not over. Discussions are well under way about linking the DS consoles to the school's wireless network to enable staff and learners to do more with the devices.

And while achieving the objective of giving their learners what they need – good basic knowledge as well as a sound grounding in literacy and numeracy – Oakdale has proved that learning and the curriculum can be leavened by innovation with technology. Dawn Hallybone concludes: 'Everything we use is chosen specifically because the teacher can link it to the curriculum'.

Notes

1 For reports on Dawn Hallybone's pioneering work with handheld devices, see: http://agentvators/580-the-innovators-15-dawn-hallybone.html (accessed 14 July 2014); http://agent4change.net/events/awards/419-teachers-in-the-frame-at-handheld-learning-09-awards.html (accessed 14 July 2014).
2 Oakdale Junior School: www.oakdalejuniors.co.uk (accessed 14 July 2014).
3 Pokemon: Typing Adventure and Art Academy: www.nintendo.com/games (accessed 14 July 2014).
4 Professor Layton: http://professorlayton.nintendo.com/ (accessed 14 July 2014).
5 Redbridge Games Network: http://redbridgegamesnetwork.blogspot.co.uk/ (accessed 14 July 2014).
6 Watch Dawn Hallybone present her work at Learning Without Frontiers: www.youtube.com/watch?v=Qx9nbSK8V5w (accessed 14 July 2014).

CHAPTER

6

Essa Academy

Essa has always been, and always will be, about the learning.

Interest in the achievements of Essa Academy in Bolton, Lancashire, is so high that the school organises regular tours for visitors. There's a charge to make them sustainable, and some of the students support the visits as part of their curriculum work. It's that sort of school.

At the end of the tour, visitors are handed iPads on which to record their opinions. Subscribing to this service ensures a steady stream of emails littered with superlative comments from all sorts of sources. It makes that sort of impression.

Essa has made a big impression on media visitors too. The only problem is that many of them see it as a technology story, an Apple story about the school that pioneered the use of iPods and iPads. However, the Essa story is a classic example of school improvement through a vision for learning that has personalisation at its heart.

Headteacher Showk Badat, who left the school in December 2013, kept charts on his office wall to show value for money in every department in his 900-pupil school. The graph for each curriculum subject matches A–C grades against what it cost to achieve them.

'They show that the costs of getting grades A, B and C are getting smaller,' he explained. 'What appears to be a high level of cost for a particular resource, ICT, gives us a high impact on grades so it has given us better value for money.'

In 2009 the cost per C+ grade was approximately £3,990 and the use of ICT brought that down to £2,380 by 2010 – a saving of £1,610 (40 per cent).

At a time of restricted budgets in schools, this is important evidence for a high-profile school that has become known for giving all its students and all its staff – not just teachers – iPod Touches first time around, and then iPads (teachers also have MacBook Air laptops). It demonstrates that ICT (including mobile devices) is a cost-effective investment.

Learning and teaching, and the released potential of its learners, are what drive the Essa Academy. The technology supports, enables and extends that. School director Abdul Chohan says that observers sometimes make the mistake that the Essa story is just about ICT.

'Essa has always been, and always will be, about the learning'

'Essa has always been, and always will be, about the learning,' he said.

> We wanted to move the organisation to where we are flexible enough to respond to the needs of students. The technology is an enabler, a digital pencil case, and it's a window to the world. It's a catalyst that speeds up learning and allows accessibility. So a learner who comes from Afghanistan, for example, or speaks Farsi or Urdu, can use the technology to communicate, to Google information, to learn and to take part. I believe that the reason it is so successful is because the solution we put into practice is mobile. Because it is mobile it is personalised. Students download applications for immediate learning – that's not so simple with generic laptops. The devices go home with them so they can capture their thoughts in the evening or even on their way home on the bus. That has become a powerful tool.

The iPods, as personal devices, were seen as crucial in capturing the 'third space' between home and school and for increasing electronic communications between students and staff to help build relationships further. Even the headteacher had to field regular email queries from students.

iPads are not seen as so personal. They are personalised to a department and to teachers, and Essa is more likely to have class/curriculum sets than issue one per pupil.

Ofsted judged Essa's leadership as 'outstanding'

Recognition of Essa's success has been swift. In an Ofsted inspection in June 2011 (2014 inspectors were in at the time of going to press), Essa was judged as 'good' in every category apart from leadership, where it was 'outstanding', and in July 2011 the school won the Outstanding ICT Learning Initiative or Partnership category of the *TES* Schools Awards.[1]

It's important to understand that Essa Academy is at the start of its learning journey rather than the end. This started in 2009 at the former Hayward School as it struggled to stay out of special measures. The intervention of sponsor Essa Foundation[2] led the move to academy status and the poor state of the buildings, and the high cost of their maintenance, necessitated inclusion in the Building Schools for the Future (BSF) programme[3] for a new build.

This was the green light for Showk Badat to begin the change management programme that, in October 2011, led students and staff into the fabulous new BSF building currently taking shape alongside what used to be Hayward. It was designed to maximise the use of ICT and features a theatre complete with three-dimensional projection.

The changes at Essa involve conceptual shifts which are deep and radical, and tie closely to the use of instant, mobile technology. Take, for example, the perceptions of students and of teachers' professional practice.

Students are not viewed as people to be shaped to 'fit' school. The individual 'space' they occupy is worked on by staff to remove any of the obstacles to their creativity or their learning. This could be the curriculum, and at Essa the curriculum has been changed to include as much choice as possible so that it fits the students rather than the other way around.

Showk Badat is critical of the current management practice of observing teachers to ensure that up to 75 per cent of teaching is 'good or better'. He feels that this is irrelevant for those children who may experience the 25 per cent 'less than good' teaching for 100 per cent of their time at school, and worries about the 'misery' that experience can cause for children who are subsequently turned off learning. So teachers at Essa are viewed through the prism of the students' learning experiences and this has resulted in richer, more effective staff development – and happier students.

Development plans take too long to implement – change is rapid

Essa isn't a place for development plans – these take far too long to implement. Take the registration process, for example. All the staff take registration. This means that all the 'significant adults' – catering staff, for example – have an interest in the learners, and the registration groups are smaller. Registration on iPod means that it can take place anywhere, maybe outside on the plaza on a sunny day. A quick group email via iPod can easily set that up. The attendance data goes straight from the iPods into the school's SIMS management system.

Showk Badat talks of training as 'reculturing', of changing mindsets. This can be seen in Year 7, where the new intake of learners get to grips with pedagogy that originated in Australia and is known as New Basics.[4] This is where they get to grips with what he calls 'real-life' learning and pursue the learning rather than a structured curriculum.

In New Basics they get to work on a rich learning topic for up to nine weeks. One of the most important is an exploration of British identity and it involves the students in all sorts of research and enquiry, sometimes visiting outlying communities. It's no coincidence that their teachers have been recruited from local primary schools.

It's easy to interpret this as a cross-curricular approach of the primary experience, but Showk Badat says, 'It's pedagogy I'm after, not content, and primary teachers are experts in personalisation. We want a curriculum more grounded in reality rather than cross-curricular.' So forget the familiar labels and tick-boxes of current practice: when students follow the learning they may well go naturally into history, or English or maths, but not because that was necessarily the intention.

The effect on the learners is palpable and they are bursting to tell you about their learning (Ofsted graded it as 'outstanding'), and how the iPods are great tools for the note-taking, research and communication along the way. They are also happy to tell you about the excellent apps they find and share with their teachers. One Year 7 girl came across eClicker[5] and took it to her teacher, who immediately adopted it for collaborative classroom work – many schools pay significant sums of money to carry out this work with pupil response technology.

This app, which is free for education, allows pupils to send their answers and contributions to shared activities on the class plasma screen. They even design their own quizzes. The student's class teacher remains unfazed because her students bring her lots of other apps and ideas. The students even run their own Genius Bar[6] to help each other (they were trained by Apple's own in-store 'geniuses').

Major savings have been made on the costs of paper and printing

While the learning drives the use of technology, there have been significant side benefits. A year before the iPods were distributed, the school printed more than a million sheets of paper. When the iPods went out there was an immediate 50 per cent drop in printing. And further savings were made when the new building opened and many of the old printers were converted for 'scan-to-email'. There are technology savings too. In the past two years there have been no requests for class sets of laptops.

What the new building brought is what Abdul Chohan calls a transformation to the full Mac environment as the managed ICT service moved away from Windows. He feels that students and staff have only scratched the surface so far and that Mac desktop applications will generate a revolution in the quality and quantity of the curriculum materials the school generates. Teachers can use the creative software tools on their MacBooks, in particular iBooks Author, to create excellent and appealing curriculum materials for their students. They upload these to Apple's free online subscription service iTunes U, from where they are downloaded to students' portable devices.

In this way the students get materials that have been personalised specially for them, and which can be updated at any time by teachers and synced again by the students.

Essa, like other schools, is judged on its results, and the evidence so far has been impressive. Prior to 2009 the school was getting 28 per cent five A stars to Cs, including English and maths, which improved all the way up to 100 per cent five A stars to C. Showk Badat commented, 'It's the same staff and it's not a magic curriculum thing – English is still English and maths is still maths. It's a sense that anything is possible – and we have still got a long way to go.'

The school is happy to share the insights from its success with other school communities and educators. However, you can be sure that the technology will not run away with the learning, as the 'reculturing' continues to be inspired by Showk Badat's exhortation that teachers should 'Feel, see, act, reflect, remove the rubble and drink tea!' For Abdul Chohan that 'rubble' will definitely include outdated technology and practices.

It's what enables the children to help run their school and it's why the list of visitors is long and illustrious. Next on the schedule was a visit by Princess Badiya of Jordan and her advisers.

Perhaps the single-mindedness with which Essa has pursued its goals for learning is best reflected in Showk Badat's remarks when he won the Social Award at the Learning Without Frontiers[7] event. 'There is no such thing as curriculum police,' he said, referring to fears to innovate the curriculum. 'I say to my staff "Do what is right for the children. It doesn't matter what our politicians feel or say".' He may have left the building but that will remain a central tenet of the senior management team.

Notes

1 *TES* schools annual awards (www.tesawards.co.uk/) recognise and reward the work of individual and teams of teachers.

2 Essa Foundation (www.essaacademy.org/) is an education charity set up to encourage research, development and introduction of best practice across schools and the curriculum, for use by headteachers, staff, governing bodies and students in schools in the UK and worldwide.

3 Building Schools for the Future (BSF) was an ambitious £55 billion secondary school rebuilding and renovation programme in England, put in place by the Blair Government. It was overseen by Partnership for Schools, a non-departmental joint venture between the Department for Children, Schools and Families (now the Department for Education), Partnerships UK and private-sector partners. BSF was controversially axed in 2010 by the incoming Education Secretary, Michael Gove, with the explanation that 'it was wasteful and bureaucratic'.

4 The New Basics curriculum is said to be 'transdisciplinary' and 'futures-oriented' as it allows students to cover all areas of knowledge at GCSE level and beyond, while tackling real-life issues such as organising community events (www.eqa.edu.au/site/forwardtonewbasics.html; accessed 14 July 2014).

5 eClicker is an iPad app that allows teachers to conduct formative assessments with students in their classroom, collect individual responses and summarise class results. These can then be shared and students can receive feedback on their own responses, later reviewed by the teacher: http://eclicker.com/ (accessed 14 July 2014).

6 Genius Bar is the technology support station found in every retail store owned by American technology giant Apple. Employees are trained and certified at the Genius Bar to offer help to customers with their Apple hardware and software: www.apple.com/uk/retail/geniusbar/ (accessed 14 July 2014).

7 Learning Without Frontiers (www.learningwithoutfrontiers.com/) was conceived in 2004 as an annual gathering of education innovation which included a conference and awards ceremony. It closed in 2013.

7

Cramlington Learning Village

You are restricted if you haven't got the technology that can come with you.

With a first-rate reputation for a pioneering 'learning to learn' programme that places as much emphasis on teaching students how to become good learners as it does on curriculum subjects, it is not surprising that staff at Cramlington Learning Village[1] have grabbed, and held on to, the harness of technology in their drive to transform education.

But there is no assumption, either implicit or explicit, that the ICT incorporated into a traditional teaching structure, will transform learning. These teachers have long understood that the effects of technology are maximised 'if it accompanies new thinking on teaching and learning', says assistant headteacher Phil Spoors.

So a journey that began around ten years ago and has continued through leadership changes has resulted in a 2,300-pupil school with mission-critical technology built around a learner-centred strategy with accelerated learning styles based on the 'small is beautiful' concept. That's why this Northumberland secondary school to the north of Newcastle upon Tyne employs three full-time web designers who build and manage the school's intranet. This is the centre of the learning experiences and a storehouse for a variety of resources linked to learning styles.

Each learning topic is connected to previous work and resources include films, video clips and audio commentaries put together by teachers to share with colleagues and, when appropriate, with parents and students. This cohesive whole-school approach, built on a common system, means teachers and students are confident they can access these resources wherever they are, in or outside the school.

Cramlington is split into a campus of three learning villages to create smaller, more manageable 'flexible learning environments' where young people aged 11–18 study, usually in groups of four around large circular tables with two PCs on each. Since 2011 there has been an ICT toolkit which includes giving each student at the start of Year 7 a personal 7-inch Android-based Samsung Galaxy tablet computer for use in the classroom and at home.

'We are trying to encourage an inquiry-based curriculum and a project-based curriculum to develop independence in our students,' explains Phil Spoors, who is also responsible for elearning. 'That's quite hard to do if students want to move around and work in groups in the classroom and then you say to them, "But actually when you use the technology you need to go and sit over there, because that's where the computer is". That's kind of defeating the purpose of having that flexible environment.'

The 'classrooms' at Cramlington are mostly set up as large open spaces where the students can move around and reconfigure the space. And then there is the large break-out area they call 'the big street', which is heavily used for small-group activities such as role play or for making videos, so it makes sense that staff would want the technology to do the same. And that, confirms Phil Spoors, is what a mobile device provides.

> It allows students to move around and interact with each other anywhere in the classroom and, unlike a computer, they are on instantly; you don't have to wait for it to boot up. You are restricted if you haven't got the technology that can come with you – you'll have to stay in the classroom or in an ICT suite.

> The tablets allow us a lot more potential for field trips and going out of school, with students being able to digitally capture what they are doing when they are out. They are also very intuitive and very easy to pick up even if the students haven't used them before.

An example of this is the school's project fortnight where all students in Years 7, 8 and 9 go out of school at some point over two weeks. During this time away from their usual learning environment, they are challenged to produce something for an exhibition day, to which parents and members of the public are invited.

Following the idea of an existing project, students worked with Northumberland treasure trail expert Tony Lennox[2] to create a tourist guide of the area. Using the GPS facility on the Galaxy tablets, and the inbuilt cameras, they developed a 'trail', a map with photos of the different locations along the way that they could use in the guides. They also collected clues and recorded interviews with local residents which they then uploaded to a website accessible for the mobile devices.

The climax of the project, says Phil Spoors, was:

> a really professional, glossy treasure trail brochure that, without the technology, would have involved a teacher having to find the digital camera to take out with them. Only one person would have been able to take those photos, the research would have all had to be based in school and they wouldn't have been able to do daft things like using a stick to draw out their ideas in the sand on the beach, which they photographed using the Galaxy Tabs and sent straight back into school. Things like that remind you that those possibilities just didn't exist before we had the tablets.

Another group of students decided to write a book called *Not Just 'Geordie Shore'* (now available for Kindle)[3] to show off Newcastle and the surrounding areas for what they really are, highlighting the things that visitors can do while touring the area. They didn't want people to think of Newcastle and its environs as the version portrayed by the inhabitants of the popular MTV *Geordie Shore* reality show, which they felt misrepresented the area.

Using the tablets to gather information and photographs in much the same way as for the treasure trail tourist guide, they self-published a book using the Lulu. com online service.[4] They have marketed this themselves and it is now stocked in tourist offices around the north-east and on Amazon.

'The good thing,' says Phil Spoors, 'is that people are placing orders through Lulu online so the students can see the books actually being sold – it has been bought by people, it's been used by people and the quality is fantastic. We used the Galaxy Tablets, but it doesn't matter what the equipment is. It could be any other tablet; it just needed to be a portable device.'

(It's worth bearing in mind that Cramlington doesn't consider itself an 'Android school' and remains interested in other technologies that suit its infrastructure and budget.)

Phil Spoors has many examples of these types of project, only made possible by the school's strong belief in developing independent learners through a mix of educational styles. For example, using enquiry-based learning with the appropriate technology, students could learn independently without intervention from their teachers.

The school also chose the Galaxy Tablet device because of the ease of access to apps. They could create their own educational ones, as well as students being able to download those that were free, and, of course, useful.

'We've now got a whole host of apps that we've created ourselves which we think really enhances what happens in the classroom and we get students to download their own from the Market,' explains Phil Spoors pointing to the vocabulary, connectives, openers, punctuation (VCOP) wall they use for language work. The idea of this app is for students to have it open alongside their written work as a facility or tool to give them any support or advice they might need.

He says that when they first got the devices some staff in the English department expressed concerns that the technology would lead to less writing and reading. They've tried to combat that by, for example, making ebooks available, which pupils can read on the devices if they want an alternative to physical books. Of course there are also books available in school, and it is very common while walking around on a visit to see groups of students sitting in their home rooms reading them, something they do every Wednesday morning, according to Phil Spoors.

Even though there have been many successes with the Galaxy devices at Cramlington, there are some things that haven't worked as well as expected. Phil Spoors says they thought the Evernote app would 'really revolutionise the way that students were researching things in the junior learning village, because they've got this great facility they can use to record, tag and organise'.

What we found is students and teachers have been so used to the way they've done things in the past that people have been quite loath to move away from those things. In some sense I wonder if it is a case of 'if it's not broken, don't fix it' and people are using things that they know work and don't want to try something that might change that.

This doesn't dampen his enthusiasm however. He believes that the problem lies with the age group (Years 7 and 8) currently using the devices. 'I think that once these get to students who are doing their GCSEs, and particularly A-levels, that's when I perceive them really using tools like Evernote to record information for their exams.'

Cramlington Learning Village wanted the mobile devices made available on a universal basis for students, starting in Year 7 and moving with them up the school, and considered various devices before opting for the Samsung Galaxy. Staff believe their approach is both equitable and sustainable – the 7-inch tablets cost the school £157.50 each (there is an additional cost for insurance and accessories). They work well with the school's Frog learning platform and, with a 97 per cent opt-in from parents, who agree to contribute £10 a month for two years towards the cost of the devices, they think they made the right decision. As equality of access is paramount, where finances prohibit opting in the school intervenes.

'We work with the e-Learning Foundation[5] and have managed to secure a grant from them for £5,000 that we use to support students who can't afford the scheme to give them the devices,' says Phil Spoors. 'For the free school meals pupils we use some of the pupil premium money. And in the very rare cases when parents say they don't agree with the students having the technology, and they don't want their son or daughter to have it, in those cases we have just had to respect those wishes so we give them access to computers when they are in school so they can still do the work.'

Teachers at Cramlington have noticed increased confidence in the students' learning and Phil Spoors believes that the tablets have something to do with that. He says from the start there is engagement because youngsters love this kind of technology, and because they are slightly better at using tablets than adults – so it's a tool that empowers them. 'You can feel the current Year 7 bubbling over with excitement,' he says. 'They are so excited about getting their tablets after half-term. They can instantly say, "This is mine. It is going to help me in my learning".'

And the confidence is growing for teachers too. For them it's a shift in pedagogy and a change in practice. It has been a learning curve for staff becoming accustomed to letting students have use of the tablets in lessons. However, Phil Spoors points out that the potential is evident for all to see:

It has been quite a shift for them to actually think that students can use these devices as and when they see fit. I think there is always that little niggling worry in the back of their minds about what if they are just sitting playing a game on it. As a member of staff, being able to let go of controlling how and when devices are used is quite difficult. There are increasing numbers of lessons, though, where students are now driving the use of technology based around what they are doing in the lesson.

On the positive side he gives an example of how learners having instant access to information online compels teachers to train their students into making sense of the material they have at their fingertips. In other words, there is a bit more strategy and thinking going on behind every action and the students are benefiting from that.

That aside, staff are totally sold on students becoming more independent and taking more control for what they are doing. With this comes the acknowledgement that the mobile devices allow students to do that, as well as being a tool for capturing progress and evidence. 'This,' he thinks, 'is another way that teachers are starting to change their practice a little bit. There is a big cross-over between tablets and computers at Cramlington. The key is to give staff and students the choice. So long as the technology is used to support, engage or enhance learning, I don't mind how they use it.'

This visionary approach to learning at Cramlington had already spread to its wider school community before the arrival of the 1:1 tablet scheme. About 25 per cent of parents were regularly accessing the parent portal on the school's virtual learning environment (VLE), which contains pupils' personal learning plans and is regularly updated with progress reports on their son or daughter as well as homework details. Although there is no real independent evidence of the part, if any, played by the tablets, Phil Spoors says the school is now seeing a massive increase in the number of parents regularly accessing the VLE.

> There is no firm evidence to say that they are using the tablets to do that as it doesn't recognise what device they are going on the VLE with, but it does coincide with the tablets being in the home. My assumption is that parents are using these as well. Now we have 41–42 per cent of parents going on the VLE to look at students' work and make comments, so it's formalising the home learning.

Another bonus across the school of the 1:1 tablet initiative is how the devices support assessment and recording. At Cramlington, this is where the value of blogs is evident. With one for each class, all students have to do is upload their work, where it awaits teacher assessment and feedback, which can include video and voice recordings. And the portability of the device means teachers can access that information wherever they are.

However, this form of assessment is not at the cost of face-to-face discussions between student and teacher. 'I will still sit down with students in a lesson and say, "let's have a little look at what I wrote here and let's discuss it",' explains Phil Spoors. 'But the advantage of delivering that wealth of information electronically over paper-based assessment is that you can link to further support resources for the feedback that you've given – "Take a little look at this, go to this website, you might find out a bit more here"'.

And also, for a teacher it's difficult to capture some of the conversations that happen in the lesson which are very much formative feedback. I can record on the blog post what I am asking and what answers are given and what feedback I am giving them. Later they can have a look at that post, add their own comments and talk about how they've actually implemented the discussion we've had as a group.

So now there is a record of that conversation, which in the past would have been a conversation that may well have been forgotten, that students can keep coming back to and you can keep coming back to as well. Being able to assess your own learning and performance makes you a reflective practitioner.

As with all schools, Cramlington has a rigorous home–school agreement around the use of ICT equipment. This general safety advice is tailored for the tablets, and online training materials are freely available for parents. Even with all the safeguards in place, the devices are fairly open for the students and they can play games on them, and listen to music, so long as they are not doing it in lesson time.

Phil Spoors expects that in five years everybody will have access to a device that allows them to support and enhance learning – whatever that may be – freeing up the curriculum and also making the relationship between teachers and students richer and more productive.

'Actually,' he says, 'what we would like to see is a change to the structure of the whole curriculum. So in Years 7 and 8 it would be lovely to think that we could have students working on more projects, becoming more independent and organised and capturing that progress throughout those projects. We could have one teacher with fewer students for more time, so you get to see the students and build those relationships, and I think that these [mobile devices] are one of the things that can support that kind of change.'

Success with its innovative learning and teaching fires Cramlington's ambitions as mobile technology becomes cheaper and easier to manage. It continues its shift to new ways of learning, reflected in other schools too, and enabled, but not driven, by the technology. Staff are keen to continue a process of change they clearly feel has barely started.

Notes

1 Cramlington Learning Village: www.cramlingtonlv.co.uk/ (accessed 14 July 2014).
2 Tony Lennox: www.treasuretrails.co.uk/ (accessed 14 July 2014).
3 Cramlington Learning Village (2012) *It's not Just Geordie Shore*. www.amazon.co.uk/Its-just-Geordie-Shore-ebook/dp/B008FDWP52 (accessed 14 July 2014).
4 See https://www.lulu.com/ (accessed 14 July 2014) for details on how to 'self-publish'.
5 The e-Learning Foundation (www.e-learningfoundation.com/) provides solutions to schools to provide equality of access for all learners.

CHAPTER

8

Woodlawn School

It's more about the learning than the teaching.

The flash flood suffered by Woodlawn School,[1] Monkseaton, in June 2012, might have been termed a disaster elsewhere. But the value of the ICT at this special school catering for around 100 pupils aged from 2 to 19 in North Tyneside resides in its staff rather than in defunct hardware.

That's because the use of ICT, and particularly mobile technology, is so firmly embedded in practice across the school that it has garnered a number of prestigious awards.[2] Given that level of expertise, a setback like the flood even opened up new opportunities when it came to buying replacement equipment.

'Woodlawn is probably the only school that I have been to where technology is "just there", where it's the norm for everyone and is used when it is the right and most effective tool – it's simply not a big deal,' explained Carol Allen, school improvement adviser for ICT and inclusion in North Tyneside. 'And the use of video by students and staff for the collection of evidence to assess, reflect, evaluate, celebrate and share is a very big deal indeed for good practice.'

Visitors to the school would agree. Woodlawn exploits a full range of technology. Used across the school are cheap recording devices that can add audio support in all sorts of locations, from push-button explanations in wall displays to doorway buttons that explain to children the facilities they can expect to find on the other side of the door – for example, specialist support features available in lavatories.

'None of this mobile technology is new in a special needs school setting,' explained Carol Allen.

> It is only part of the continuum of good practice that has been here for years. Think of the 'talking tin lids' that were created to identify the contents of a tin for someone who is blind. We all grabbed them and used them for education. Those talking tin lids spawned a whole range of extremely useful and affordable talking devices for schools. They were designed as functional everyday living devices but became a huge educational success.

> Yes, we have mobile devices and want more, but it's only part of a really complex jigsaw – it's a different picture in special schools as we need to personalise, create and invent to a greater level.

It's true, handheld devices are in evidence everywhere at Woodlawn, and staff have their own iPads. Small video cameras, like the ubiquitous Flip, are used by learners and adults alike for reflective practice. Sitting in on any lesson will invariably reveal this sort of activity, with teachers as well as pupils naturally sharing the new uses they have developed for using video for instant feedback.

The range of technology use goes all the way up, from other mobile devices like the Nintendo DS (not a major success because of management issues – but there are plans to try again), iPods, iPads, Fizzbooks, Chromebooks, personal tablets to desktop PCs and specialist communication aids. They even use the Nintendo Wii and Xbox Kinect for PE and movement therapies.

A walk around the school is frequently punctuated by interventions from the students who want to show what they are doing on their devices. While they are clearly enamoured with the technology, it's their learning that they are so proud of and so keen to show you.

You'll meet children from other countries who are able to get on with their work and basic communication thanks to staff pointing them in the direction of Google Translate on the mobile devices. Headteacher Simon Ripley explained,

> We've got a Polish lad who, through the wifi, was able to translate using Google Translate from Polish to English and one of his friends would sit next to him and try to do it from English to Polish to really support his language from the early stages because when he came here he had no English other than 'Yes' or 'No'. From a global point of view it's great because the other kids are picking up another language as well. But that really supported his English language development and throughout the school that was seen as a success story.

This student was provided with his own iPad for this purpose by an external service. And this is not an isolated example. One new student could only speak Shona, so they found an app that could translate the 50 most commonly used words, which was a great start to developing her language skills.

It's fair to say that the school has a 'by any means' policy – it will use virtually any technology that benefits its learners and teachers. These could be devices designed for specific needs, off-the-shelf technology from the high street and even end-of-line sale goods from the supermarket. Learners at Woodlawn have a wide range of needs so there is no 'one size fits all' and no plans for a 1:1 implementation, although devices increasingly go home with students.

The standout feature at Woodlawn, however, is the way teachers' confidence with technology frees them up to find new uses. Like Cat Findlay, who on our visit was using the Aurasma 'augmented reality' app[3] on an iPod to make students' wall displays interactive by embedding quick response (QR) codes[4] into them. Students and visitors point their iPods or iPads at the QR codes and get immediate web access to background information about the display, for example why and how it was created, and what the process involved. This could be text, audio, graphics, photos or video – even all of them.

Simon Ripley, talking about the impact of mobile devices, said:

> One of the big things for us has been the speed at which kids can pick up a bit of kit and then do a million things in seconds. And they can freely move around the school interacting with their devices and each other. I like our kids working out of the classroom too – we have displays set up like treasure hunts using QR codes and StoryPhones[5] as well. It's more about the learning than the teaching and it can free up teachers to let the kids be more independent than they have been in the past, and with a wider range of resources.

'Mobile technology helps Woodlawn give learners more access and participation', said Simon Ripley. As a result they develop more confidence and autonomy so that they have greater control of their learning, allowing their teachers to help them even more.

This applies equally to the teachers and support staff; their practice is reflective and the mobiles are valuable in producing evidence of their learning and allowing them to share it far more fluently – for example, between home and school – than they were previously able.

'The phrase is, "it's a shorter workflow",' explained Carol Allen. 'If you are a really busy and committed practitioner, anything which is a shorter workflow you will use more frequently than something that has a longer or more complex work-flow.'

That evidence is also important for other professionals, she said:

> You have concrete evidence for sharing with other professionals. If you take, for example, the early speech development in a child with developmental issues – you can try and transcribe, or you can mark it on a tick list, but it's not the same as seeing a little sample of video of that child and where he or she is up to. You can be sitting with a parent and you could race through and record a bit of what is happening in that classroom, come back and discuss it. And you are doing it in real time for reflection and evaluation and multi-professional working.

This level of professional involvement also says a lot for the local authority's commitment to hold on to its advisory staff, against a national trend which has seen many schools stripped of this kind of support.

Woodlawn has also purchased the Iris Connect classroom system[6] for recording, analysing and sharing classroom practice (online too), but has not fully integrated its use yet. It is hoped that this will take classroom observation, again using video to capture evidence and reflect on it, only this time for teachers' professional development – something all staff and learners are already comfortable with – to a higher level.

Also important are relevance and engagement, and a sense of fun. 'Kids should enjoy being in the school and what I find the most interesting is if you give the kids a 15-minute free choice on the iPad they always go on Maths Ninja,'[7] explained Simon Ripley,

> It's a free app and it looks rubbish but educationally it's spot-on and the kids just go on it because it's fun and it's hidden learning, and you get that with many games. Last year it was PopMath,[8] which had a display, and basically the kids would compete to get the highest scores – a bit like the cookery programme *Ready, Steady, Cook*. The kids were absolutely over themselves to get to the top – stunning. Fun and relevant.

The mobile revolution spearheaded by Apple's iPods and iPads has reached Woodlawn and these and other devices are being used and continuously evaluated. But there is no one technology 'silver bullet' in a school like this, where staff are focused on stimulating and engaging their learners with whatever tools are most effective.

Android tablets are also being considered, and adviser Carol Allen was one of the first educators to start using Tesco's low-cost Hudl tablet, which she considers great value for money.[9]

While the range of needs at Woodlawn might preclude a 1:1 project of standard devices, the school still has to deal with management of software and apps, as in any other school, albeit with a greater range. 'At the start it was all about free apps, which was great,' said Simon Ripley. 'But we are now at a point where we are starting to spend on them because free doesn't always mean great.' And Apple's devices are still creating syncing issues. However, the economics are sustainable and there is no fear that the level of investment will have to be cut back.

Integrating the range is producing rich learning experiences:

> One of the big things for us is to get the kids doing interactive presentations. They start by taking photographs during the lessons and then plotting them into a presentation. At the end of the lesson they put it on the board and talk about it. We did this kind of thing in the past with Flip video cameras where we would get the kids to record what they were doing and discuss their productions at the end of the lesson.

While one of Woodlawn's priorities for the future is to develop greater involvement of parents, the top one remains to open up further opportunities for its learners. 'What I really want to do is put it on to the kids,' stressed Simon Ripley. 'I want them to become much more independent – within their own needs – deciding the learning journeys in their lesson. So you give them a little problem or a question or something they need to work on independently, as far as possible, to get to the end result with minimal support. That's the real challenge for me.'

The school also hopes to embrace app development, working with partners like the Culture Lab at Newcastle University,[10] to create its own solutions. 'They are doing a project at the minute around voice loudness modulation using an app for kids with cerebral palsy because they struggle with the voice modulation,' said

Simon Ripley. This work could involve students too, further developing the capacity for peer learning and support.

> Our IT qualifications around the senior end now include functional skills, and that is in our school development plan all the way through the school – not just in terms of IT but functional life skills. That could be taking the kids out in the community to make sure they can use the technology they find there, for example testing supermarket scanners to see whether they are suitable for people with disabilities and providing feedback that could conceivably be considered for future designs.

> One-to-one is on the horizon – it would be daft to think otherwise – but it's a case of trying to offset that against other needs. We never settle on just one thing: we bombard our learners!

And that's full of such rich learning experiences that even a flash flood can't sweep it away.

Notes

1 Woodlawn School: http://www.woodlawn.org.uk/ (accessed 14 July 2014).
2 Northern Grid For Learning Awards 2011. Woodlawn was winner in three categories: Secondary Computer Graphics and Art; Secondary Creative Digital Media; Overall Excellence in ICT. Northern Grid case study at http://www.northerngrid.org/resource/woodlawn-case-study (accessed 14 July 2014).
Naace ICT Impact Awards (2012) Supporting Inclusion in Any Phase. http://www.naace.co.uk/events/conference2012/naaceimpactawards2012/winners (accessed 14 July 2014).
3 www.aurasma.com/: The Aurasma 'augmented-reality' app was launched in 2011 with a vision 'to enable an augmented world, where every image, object and place has its own Aura'. It has more than 40,000 customers in over 100 countries.
4 Quick response (QR) code is text that has been encoded in a two-dimensional barcode format that can be read by smartphones and tablets (http://en.wikipedia.org/wiki/QR_code).
5 StoryPhones (www.storyphones.co.uk/) is an MP3 digital audio system with headsets and a remote control that primary schoolchildren can use to listen to stories, sing along to songs, join in listening games, learn new languages and even record their own stories to share.
6 Iris Connect classroom system for recording, analysing and sharing classroom practice: http://www.irisconnect.co.uk/ (accessed 14 July 2014).
7 Maths Ninja: https://itunes.apple.com/gb/app/math-ninja-hd-free!/id373814902?mt=8 (accessed 14 July 2014).
8 PopMath: https://itunes.apple.com/gb/app/id295536766?mt=8 (accessed 14 July 2014).
9 Tesco Hudl tablet: http://www.tesco.com/direct/hudl/ (accessed 14 July 2014).
10 Culture Lab at Newcastle University: http://www.ncl.ac.uk/culturelab/ (accessed 14 July 2014).

Frank Wise School

It's only by encouraging and allowing good practice that we can really take it further.

Frank Wise School[1] is a very special sort of special school, long known for its use of technology in meeting the extremely broad range of learning needs of its pupils. It is led by a special sort of headteacher, too.

Sean O'Sullivan is a one-time winner of the Becta ICT in Practice Award[2] for secondary inclusion (in 2003). Under his leadership the school has worked hard to embrace the learning opportunities that technology can bring.

He is also an Apple Distinguished Educator[3] which, although a recognition of his expertise with that brand, does not necessarily indicate a bias towards any particular technology, but rather an interest in what it can do for the children in his care. However, as Apple has often been at the forefront of technological innovation, it is with them that he chooses to work. 'The iPad is still streets ahead in terms of the quality of the tool coupled with the enormous range of apps that you can run on it,' he says of the company's product. The iPad is proving very popular in special needs contexts, not least because of its accessibility and ease of use for people with disabilities of any sort.

This is a feature that is important in a school that serves a large chunk of north Oxfordshire and accepts children with a very wide variety of special educational needs. Some students are on the autistic spectrum, while others have conditions such as Down syndrome[4] or cerebral palsy. All have learning difficulties; although one or two are achieving GCSEs, others remain at very early cognitive levels throughout their school careers, working at what are known as P Levels (meaning 'pre–National Curriculum'). However, all are taught within age groups, so classes are mixed–ability and students are expected to work with, and support, each other.

'Technology is always moving at such a rapid pace,' Sean O'Sullivan explains. He is particularly impressed with the developments that tablets such as the iPad offer. 'The fact that it's a touchscreen, and the design of the interface is so intuitive, means that for the vast majority of our children it's a step forward.'

It is this directness, of simply touching what you want to interact with, with no need for peripherals such as a mouse or keyboard to make things happen, that makes handheld devices so attractive.

This isn't true for all students however. 'There are one or two for whom it's actually less successful than a conventional route, as it were, and obviously you have to take account of that,' he acknowledges. However, as is often recognised, making technology more usable for some people often has a knock-on effect for everyone.

But it's the classic scenario that what's generally good for children in our setting is also a good development for everybody. We've seen touchscreen technology move out of the cloistered environment of the special-needs environment into some big-hitting mainstream areas – such as airport kiosks and shopping malls – to rapid development with the smartphones and iPhones.

When they first got going you were suddenly seeing a niche concept – touchscreen technology – hitting a universal market. You just needed the right technology combined with the insightful design of the software programmers to make everybody need this way forward.

This shift, from specialist to generic, from meeting the needs of a small group to those of the whole population, has meant that prices have fallen and understanding has risen. Sean O'Sullivan adds, 'The spin-off has been that it now brings those tools back into the hands of kids in special schools in a way that we could never have pushed forwards with when it was our own technology designed for people with special needs.'

As a result, a lot of the stigma has been lifted from using a technology that marked the user out as different. 'The children perceive it as a desirable item, a funky tool', he believes, a shift from previously, where 'there was always that nagging feeling that, "Well, I've got this but everyone else uses one of those". Well, that's completely gone now.'

It's not just design that has created such an interest within the special educational needs community, it is also the portability of the devices. As Sean O'Sullivan points out, teachers no longer have to take children to devices – such as PCs plugged into walls, or larger items like interactive whiteboards or plasma boards – and then make accommodations and adaptations to enable them to use the equipment.

Mobile technology turns this on its head. Children can now remain wherever they are best positioned, and devices can be quickly and easily brought to them. Even when the setting doesn't change, the position the child accesses the technology from can alter. Some children with more complex needs may need to spend time each day in particular positions for medical reasons. This could be lying horizontal for physiotherapy, sitting still to be fed by tube or standing in a supportive frame to strengthen their muscles.

The portability of mobile technology can not only make these sessions less stressful, but also enable learning to continue when, otherwise, it might be difficult or 'quite distressing and unpleasant and not something the child looks forward to'.

We've always tried to build educational activities around those. For instance, you don't just put a child into a standing position and then leave him or her. You are trying to make that a functional part of their day while you are doing something else to push their education forward. And sometimes you want technology to be part of their working day. With such motivating tools it can actually have a really striking impact on their ability to cope for longer periods in positions that for them are not easy.

Sean O'Sullivan feels that there is also something exciting about what the iPad does beyond the mobility of the device. 'I think the really interesting area is the apps,' he says. 'There is an incredible creative buzz out there and the difficulty is keeping up with new and innovative tools that you can think about how to use in your setting with your children. I think sometimes it can be quite overwhelming. There are so many tools out there that trying to see the wood from the trees, so to speak, is the new problem, the new barrier.'

The students certainly feel the impact, both from their use of the tablets in school, and also from the investment in them made by families for home use. 'I always find it very reassuring that the children deal with the mixed economy of different platforms that they use,' he adds. 'Whether it is games consoles, home PC or a school-based Apple computer, they seem to find their way through all of them without really sort of pulling their hair out and wondering what is going on. They just accept that you do it differently on this thing and this is how you start this one up.'

Sean O'Sullivan also believes that the very visual nature of the interface helps.

> They are very comfortable with the iPads and don't seem to get fazed. If they've been busy in a program and maybe even unintentionally done something – like touched the home button and dropped out of the program – they either use that as an opportunity to look at something else, or if they did want to get back to it, they recall the icon.

> It is a very visual environment for them. They know where they were, they seem to know the icon and go back and carry on as if nothing much has happened. It doesn't seem to trouble them in the way that some adults can get quite panicked.

The students' use of the school iPads is certainly effortless. During break time several choose to use them for fun. Bridget in Year 9 starts with the Bloom app, a lovely combination of sounds and images that cycles through and then fades out music the user creates. Then she goes on to watch videos before snatching a photo of one of her friends. David from her class is equally adept. He plays the on-screen drum kit, then watches *SpongeBob SquarePants* on YouTube. He has also been using the MadPad app and shows off what he has created.

MadPad is an app that records a moment of sound and video – a cough, a word, a clicked finger, a clinking teaspoon – which then forms the basis of an on-screen musical composition. Just touching any one of their icons replays the content. A sequence can be recorded to form an intriguing piece of music with images. In one clip another student, Ted, has even managed to catch someone at the point of sneezing.

Some of these apps are brought into the curriculum, some are just for fun and entertainment. There are other uses too, principally as a communication aid.

In the sixth form, five students bring in their own iPads with Proloquo2Go loaded. This app is very flexible in the way it supports communication. While it can be used with text and an on-screen keyboard, more often it provides a screen of symbols, icons that represent words and phrases that will build into sentences to be 'spoken' by the machine.

Communication is one of two main reasons Sean O'Sullivan believes parents buy iPads for students, either directly themselves, or with the help of charities. For children with more profound needs, parents see that 'it may help the child to improve the ability to interact with the world around them,' whereas for 'those with communication needs they can use the tool to actually express themselves'.

The iPad is a device designed for individual use, a very personal machine, so there are advantages to students having their own. 'Where parents have been able to provide them individually, that's been fantastic because it can be personal to the child and customised,' says Sean O'Sullivan. He explains: 'If it is their own iPad their photo library contains photos relevant to them, their communication software is tailored to meet their needs, and the vocabulary is appropriate to them.'

The devices have also helped pupils demonstrate their abilities in quite startling ways. 'The one I was stunned by was a pupil using a DJ app,' says Sean O'Sullivan. 'It gives you a virtual pair of decks on screen, and there's a physical double-deck that you can connect to the iPad. This child is totally blind. He wouldn't have been able to perceive the visual interface on a flat touchscreen, but using the physical deck with two turntables that you can move and "scratch" with and buttons here and there, he was able to directly affect the playing of the music.'

What so impressed him was not that this boy could manipulate the decks, but that the degree of his engagement and his response to the activity were more than would have been expected.

> It was remarkable to see not only how engaged he was with the activity, but how much difference it made in terms of the quality of the sound. There was one bit where he was working with a heavy-metal track and he was really getting active and moving more quickly in all respects. When the member of support staff working with him suggested they change a few tracks and put on a couple of bluesy, slower ones his entire method of interaction with the music changed and he appeared to be more pensive and much slower with it. I was really taken aback by it.

A girl in hospital could keep in touch with her classmates via iPads using their built-in and easy-to-use video-conferencing software, FaceTime: 'The students all got a huge amount out of it, without all the rigmarole of making a special trip out. Can we all squeeze into the minibus? Can we fit into the hospital room? It made communication at a distance much more straightforward.'

The iPads are also being used for more formal learning activities across the curriculum, although not yet in the same spontaneous way that they are used for relaxation.

'I've seen children using tools on the iPad like Photo Booth,' explains Sean O'Sullivan, talking about an app that comes with the device that allows users to grab quick photos and videos of themselves or others. 'That's just a fun environment to record themselves talking to camera, just messing about. At other times they are using it within a lesson to do a very quick clip to say what their opinion of something is, or talking out loud about how they tried to do a maths calculation or something like that.'

The problem is that these are seen as discrete uses of the iPad rather than simply as part of the lesson. 'But,' says Sean O'Sullivan, 'I think they see those tools as linked to the iPad. This is the sort of thing you can do with the iPad, but they don't so readily get encouraged to use it as a recording tool. I think that's a big area for development for us. Getting people to recognise what you can do with it as a creative tool as opposed to just something that is full of apps that you can just explore things with.'

All sorts of imaginative uses are making their way into classrooms. In science lessons, for instance, an app for measuring sound was used. A large loudspeaker had small polystyrene beads scattered on it, then different styles of music were played at varying volumes. The students noted what happened to the beads against the readings on the on-screen meter. This made the changes tangible for them so they could perceive the differences, and they could predict what might happen if the music was faster or louder.

Higher up the school, in the sixth form, handhelds and mobiles are being used as a way for students to gather evidence systematically for their City and Guilds qualifications.

> They've been using smartphones along with digital cameras, but looking at specifically recording still photos and video clips and then cross-referencing those as evidence of what the children are achieving in terms of their targets and so on.

Head of sixth form Dean Cooke sees immediate benefits from using the tablets' cameras. 'As PE coordinator I encourage staff to take the iPad to lessons to give immediate feedback.' One very helpful use has been giving students a way to critique their own performance: 'Gymnastics is aesthetic. You can review the image. This is an instant thing.'

Craig Clarke, the Year 9 teacher, agrees, as you can 'watch it straight back on the screen', whereas previously staff would have to use a camcorder to record the activity, then review it on the interactive whiteboard in another lesson. He's used the same approach in science, recording the process of an experiment, then playing it back at the end of the lesson to remind the students of what they did.

As the sixth formers are moving towards personal independence, these devices support the process. For instance, the students hold discussion groups. Recently they debated whether the police should be armed. They split into small groups for research, aided by the iPads, then came back together to put across their various points of view.

There are also more practical research tasks. Once a week sixth formers eat out at one of Banbury's cafes. Using the devices they can read the menus online beforehand, check the prices, decide where to go and, for some, plan a route to get there.

These trips into town are opportunities for some students to practise travelling independently. The school has two mobile phones equipped with GPS to support this and students are instructed to phone the school from key points to keep staff informed. Although the technology allows staff to plot students' progress on an on-screen map, this is something they haven't found the need to implement yet.

Smartphones are also part of Sean O'Sullivan's thinking for recording pupils' work at school. For a number of years the school has used digital cameras for photos and videos, but the smartphone is increasingly viewed as a more versatile tool for adults.

> There are advantages to having it in your hand. It can be just quick and easy in that context of capturing children involved in their work without thinking that all the time you've got to be carrying your camera around. It's a bit like wearing a watch. It's part of your battery of tools that you have as an adult.

The increasing ease of use of handheld devices has created, paradoxically, one of the issues Sean O'Sullivan thinks should be tackled when embedding handheld and mobile technology at Frank Wise. Staff are comfortable with the use of digital media and technologies already present in school practice, but iPads are a disruption as they offer alternative, more immediate ways of working that can open up fresh learning opportunities. Why and how should teachers move on?

As with the introduction of previous new generations of devices into the school, they have taken an approach of trying it out first to see what it will do before rolling it out widely.

> We are following the same pattern of piloting ideas, sharing good practice and trying to encourage cross-fertilisation between people, asking, 'How did you do that?' or, 'I could do that on mine.' But to get it embedded over the long term requires some kind of shorter and medium-term process that sets about trying to point out what the opportunities are.

Compulsion, he believes, doesn't work:

> I think if we were rating everyone through a new appraisal policy – 'You must be seen to use your iPad twice a day,' that sort of thing – it would fall flat on its face. It's only by encouraging and allowing good practice that we can really take it further.

This gradual approach involved simply supplying iPads to each class and seeing what they made of them. There are three iPads to a class – typically eight or nine children – and teachers are encouraged to use them as personal devices.

The theory is that when staff see technology as something personal, they learn about it and what they can do with it, a belief backed up by experience from various schemes over the years. However, things have not worked out quite as expected.

'I was assuming that was going to be an absolute no-brainer,' says Sean O'Sullivan. 'There have been several classes where the staff have felt that because they've got a laptop anyway, "I don't need to dedicate an iPad just to me; I can just use it now and again".'

Sean O'Sullivan can empathise with the staff who are perhaps reticent about discovering what these devices can do, as his own already established use of technology can bring challenges.

> Even with something straightforward like word processing, I think you go through a learning period. I use Pages on an Apple laptop and I struggle when I am on a train trying to write a document in Pages app on the iPad. I go through that classic scenario, 'But where's the . . . ?' 'Why can't I . . . ?' 'How do you do this . . . ?' The tools are there but they look different, and I don't recognise them.

Even though the approach seems quite casual, the implementation process remained the responsibility of the senior leadership team, encouraged by Sean O'Sullivan. Deputy head Simon Knight handles the practicalities of getting the iPads into people's hands and up and running, and coordinating workshops for sharing good practice.

However, there is a growing appreciation that implementation can be more effective when responsibilities for innovation in teaching and learning with new technologies are shared, and not delivered through a top-down management approach. 'We've moved from initially Simon controlling the iPads and delivering a single set of apps to each one, to a voucher-based system,' Sean O'Sullivan explains. With a 'modest budget', staff recommendations on how to spend it are very welcome.

The balance is shifting, Sean O'Sullivan reflects, as instances of demand from the grassroots grow. Despite this movement, he believes there is a further stage yet – where classes are not only doing interesting things with the iPads, but would be up in arms at the prospect of them not being replaced: 'I can see some fantastic opportunities that we absolutely have to have access to.'

The signs are already there. One of the younger members of staff, in her first year of teaching, wanted to explore the possibilities of iBooks authoring to write on-screen books for her class to use on the iPads (they are synced via iTunes U). 'The recycled laptop that she had from a member of staff who moved on wasn't capable of working with iBooks Author to create materials,' explains Sean O'Sullivan, 'so she made a case and now she has the newest laptop in the whole school as opposed to one of the oldest. Harriet is an example of "I can't move forward with what I want to do unless you give me the tools".' It is this pressure from the bottom up that he believes will provide a greater degree of success.

He sees few issues with the policy of individual staff managing the machines in their own classroom.

> It's a modest number of tools in each class. It's easy for them to keep on top of things like charging and synchronising and so on. If we had a huge number, there might be consideration about ways of moving forward such as using boxes where you can slot in 20 iPads at a time and not only charge them, but synchronise them all at one go. On a larger scale, I think we would be presented with different challenges, but at the scale we are working at it seems very manageable.

Another practicality of using devices that are designed to spend much of their time online is that of esafety, something Sean O'Sullivan says is no different when using iPads. 'Generally speaking, an awful lot of what we want to try and do with the children is about teaching them strategies for coping,' he says, 'both protective behaviours in the first place, and what to do if something unacceptable happens, to try and give them that kind of independent strategy. Like, "If I take charge of this how do I know there's a problem and what do I do about the problem?"'

Use of these devices at Frank Wise School improves the possibility of students becoming independent with technology despite the challenges of their learning needs. As well as the usability of tablets, the cost and portability mean that the time when all students will have such a device is moving closer.

'Things have got tighter and tighter financially,' says Sean O'Sullivan, 'but we have managed to get to a point where the lower cost of items like handheld technology means that we can provide more stuff in the class so children have more access to technology when they need it than ever before, in our setting.

> I think the other thing is that, because of its increased accessibility – the more intuitive interface – I get a feeling that staff are more comfortable in letting children run with it than they used to be with conventional systems such as a laptop or a desktop computer where I think there was always a background fear of 'What if a child does something that trashes the work or the system? It will take us a while to get things back to where they should be.' So I think there may be slight increases in opportunities just because the adults are giving more opportunities.

Cost is not the only factor that makes 1:1 (students having their own devices) a more attractive option for Frank Wise students: 'The huge advantage of 1:1 is, of course, that they could take devices home as well. An awful lot of our learners come to school in taxis and minibuses, so issues of security during that journey home would be fairly minimal.' However, despite falling prices, it is not affordable yet.

So the focus remains on greater use in school:

> I think probably the area I am interested in is, what can we do that gets children using them as a more creative tool? The iPad in particular has real strengths here. While it is a little unwieldy as a camera, it is a very decent environment for tweaking things like a video edit. The challenge, I think, for children with iPhones and iPod Touch and so on is that while it might be a more easily managed device for capturing photos and video, I think it's a really difficult environment to then manipulate those media and edit things and share them. Not by any means impossible, but harder and, for some of our children, too hard.

Regardless of any difficulties, Sean O'Sullivan believes the use of these devices is only just beginning.

> I would like to see a lot more children being encouraged to just use those tools within their day-to-day work to make things. To record themselves or their friends doing things, and recognising that it has a place. For a long time we've been quite good about putting digital cameras in their hands and not being too precious about the possible damage to the camera, so the concept of children being the creators of the media – I think that's embedded. But I don't think people have really taken on board the full capacities of these tools to be used in that way.

Making videos is a well-established part of the work at Frank Wise School, to the extent of having a dedicated space with high-quality equipment, including the latest technologies. 'We have got a media suite, iWise,'[5] explains Sean O'Sullivan, 'We've got iPads in there now so we have got them accessible in a context where people might think about it [using them for video]. But my perception of the practice I have seen so far is that, because we have also equipped that space with high-quality cameras, monster tripods and really substantial traditional equipment, I don't think we've taken the opportunities to explore iPads. Even in a context where you know you are deliberately trying to make a film, there is almost an aversion to it.'

It seems that, having established a level of expertise, and of expectation about the standards that are to be achieved, not necessarily in pupil outcomes but with the technology available, it is difficult to shift to another paradigm, to one that is very immediate and perhaps concerned more about content and quick response than quality. This simplicity is where the paradox lies, and it's a barrier to greater use. Staff are adept at making movies. They are comfortable with the processes embedded in school practice, but iPads represent a new way of working.

'Basically we are now film making,' says Sean O'Sullivan. 'I would say that is embedded in the curriculum and people use it in all sorts of aspects of their subjects across the week. But we are in the early days of trying to embed the use of handheld tools.'

This friction between well-established ways of working and new possibilities is a source of tension. The investment that the school has made in technology over the years, and in improving the skills of teachers, has paid off in terms of teaching and learning. But having a staff confident and competent with the technology they use means they see little need to change.

'I think there is probably going to be a longer haul to get staff who are comfortable with existing technologies finding that they can do the same and more with handheld technologies,' says Sean O'Sullivan. In order to move on with the options available on the tablets he believes there needs to be a shift in thinking, so the focus is on the activity, not the high-quality end product: 'The children can do some amazing things when encouraged to use any old tools.'

Is the school too advanced in its use of technology, and hampered by its own good practice? 'We have not exactly trapped ourselves, but we are hindered by the practice that we had established,' thinks Sean O'Sullivan. There are ways of working and processes that staff are used to. But the latest technologies bring about a choice that staff have not had to deal with previously. 'I think there are lots of apps out there so you can almost find one to suit your style. But getting those tools in the hands of the children, and pointing out you can do these things with it, is still a cultural shift for some of the school.'

The upshot is that schools that had been lagging behind in their adoption of technology in the classroom are now in the position of being able to move beyond where Frank Wise School has got to. Sean O'Sullivan points out that they can come fresh to activities, as with making films, for instance 'Now you know you can make a film with the iPad then why not start doing it?' he asks. Whereas for schools like his own, staff might miss the possibilities that are now available because of the experience they have built up with more established methods. He says, 'The schools that do know how to make films might be held back by not being able to see the opportunities that the new tools present.'

Frank Wise School has always been keen to adopt new technologies and to explore how they can enhance teaching and learning for children with special educational needs. And its successes have brought numerous awards and plaudits over the years. But it seems that mobile and handheld technologies are bringing fresh challenges, even for teachers thought to be at the cutting edge.

It is an issue with several layers, as Sean O'Sullivan explains.

> I think it is partly a cultural shift, partly waiting for the tools to catch up and be as functional as they might have been on other technologies, and partly just time, of people needing to get to grips with them.

As with other technological shifts over the years, staff at Frank Wise School are rising to such challenges, always looking for the fresh opportunities that they can bring to enrich the curriculum for the children and young people in their care.

Notes

1 Frank Wise School, Banbury, Oxfordshire: http://www.frankwise.oxon.sch.uk/ (accessed 14 July 2014).
2 Becta is the UK Government's former ICT agency for education. It was closed in November 2010 by the incoming Conservative and Liberal Democrats Coalition Government in the so-called 'bonfire of the quangos'. Its awards were designed to identify and reward individuals and organisations who used ICT to support school improvement.
3 Apple Distinguished Educators (www.apple.com/uk/education/apple-distinguished-educator/) is a global community of more than 2,000 education leaders recognised by Apple as doing innovative work with the company's technology, in and out of the classroom.
4 Down syndrome, also known as Down's syndrome, is a genetic condition that causes some level of learning disability and a characteristic range of physical features: www.downs-syndrome.org.uk/ (accessed 14 July 2014).
5 The iWise media centre was opened in 2009 (www.frankwise.oxon.sch.uk). It is a state-of-the-art suite of rooms with one large teaching space and meeting room, its own cafe area, fully equipped sound studio, green-screen space and an animation studio.

10

Apps for Good

Learners taking the lead

It's not easy to engage some of the students from the farms around Wick High School in Caithness, Scotland. 'They don't like school; they are not academic; they want to live, work and breathe on a farm,' said teacher Chris Aitken.

Three of those very same boys – John, Kieran and Ryan – took an Apps for Good[1] course at their school and won a national app-making award scheme which resulted in their Cattle Manager app,[2] created to help farmers manage their herds without the distraction of cumbersome paperwork, being professionally produced. It has since earned 3.9 out of five stars from customers in the Google Play app store.

'This has been great for them,' said Chris Aitken. 'They know the problem. They know exactly what works and what doesn't work on a farm.'

Girls are supposedly a hard-to-reach group when it comes to technology. But four other Wick students, Caitlin, Beth, Rebekah and Jeri, created their own app with Apps for Good. Dog Log,[3] designed to help dog owners keep their pets trim, healthy and happy, also took a national award and is now ensconced in the Google Play store, where it has earned 4.5 points out of five.

The girls commented:

> As animal lovers and pet owners, we read about the growing problem of overweight dogs. We therefore decided to develop an app with a competitive element to help encourage young people to walk their dogs more often.

The apps even had their own glitzy launch event in London in January 2014, which also celebrated the success of all the other national Apps for Good winners. Cattle Manager, designed to let farmers read and add information about each cow on their mobile phone (including important dates, for example for injections) as they go around the farm, won the 'Power to do More – getting the most from your time' category, sponsored by Dell, while Dog Log won the 'Learning and Information – helping others learn and using information for good' category, sponsored by Thomson Reuters.

It was a public event held at Thomson Reuters in Canary Wharf in London's Docklands, and was fired with extraordinary energy as groups of young people presented their winning projects to the great and the good of the UK's education community – and, for the first time, parents too. Educators, industry leaders, journalists, policy-makers and politicians were all deeply impressed by the work of the students, their confidence and clarity in explaining their projects and the success of Apps for Good in making mobile technology the very material for highly engaging learning and entrepreneurship, and the means for communicating its own story.

The organisation, then working with more than 200 schools, some 1,700 students and more than 700 external experts, has established the importance of schools partnering with outside organisations to enrich the curriculum and create engaging and relevant 'real–world' learning experiences for real audiences. It is now embarking on international expansion.

The organisation's UK chairman is Charles Leadbeater, journalist, author and recognised expert on innovation. He told those attending the celebration:

> I would like to do this sort of thing every day. I think it would be great if every school in the country could do this work on a regular basis, and if every child could have the opportunity to learn in the way that these young people have had the opportunity to learn by finding problems, devising solutions, making and then showing them.

> There is no reason why that shouldn't be an experience that's available to every child in the country in every school, and that's what, at Apps for Good, we want to achieve, make possible.

He said that since the students' apps had been selected for professional development in 2013, the students had worked 'incredibly hard' with developers (like Novoda[4] and Plant Pot[5]) to turn them into professional products to be included in the Google Play store. 'In the process I think they have grown enormously in their ability to collaborate,' he added, 'but also in their ability to sell, to pitch, to articulate and to show how valuable it is for anyone's education to do things which aren't to do with school.'

He told the students:

> The most interesting things you do as young people are nothing to do with school; the places where you develop most are invariably not at school; the most interesting ideas come to you outside the classroom. So what we are trying to do is to provide a structured way to do that.

When students are given that structure they respond. Chris Aitken, who is the computer science teacher at Wick High School, agrees. 'The hardest part to think of was the problem to solve,' he said.

> Once that happened they just ran with it. They drove it from beginning to end. Bob Schukai [the outside expert from Thomson Reuters] gave them pointers on how to develop it, and then they went on to win the national competition.

Never has an educational programme opened up so many opportunities to students and opened up so many doors to industry as Apps for Good has. It has helped revolutionise Wick High School's Computing Science department and has had a direct effect on the uptake throughout all year groups. Students are motivated, they are proud of their ideas and achievements and get a great insight into app development from idea generation all the way through to development and marketing.

The breadth of the curriculum work is what has excited so many of those involved. Most people in education are aware of the importance of STEM (science, technology, engineering and mathematics) and how the context of this approach adds so much to the individual subjects within it. However, that context has been widened to include entrepreneurialism and design – hence the relatively new acronym, STEAMED.

This context allows work developed for Apps for Good to traverse virtually the whole curriculum. The students follow the learning provided by the project wherever it takes them. It will usually involve at least a needs survey of potential customers, number crunching for market viability and all the design and creation processes required to create a product and market it successfully.

UK managing director of Apps for Good Debbie Forster explained:

> Traditional education systems are wasting talent. Many young people are demotivated by traditional teaching methods that leave them ill prepared for the real world. Technology is advancing, exciting the imagination of young people who want to use it to make, play and share. We believe that technology can be a great equaliser and a massive force for good to transform lives and communities anywhere around the world.

Debbie Forster is inspired by the development of STEAMED. She said:

> Yes, STEM is important. But where are the arts, the entrepreneurialism? Where is the design? Where is the life in that? And people want it. We don't give schools 'This is how you do Apps for Good'. We give them a broad road map, and then we say, 'Do what you do best.'

> If you do STEAMED I defy you to find a young person who can't find a way into it. And I defy you to find an industry that couldn't draw from it. And within it is what our generation needs.

Further relevance and engagement come from the use of external experts. Bob Schukai perhaps exemplifies this best. The laid-back American, who lives in Atlanta and has an office in New York, is global head of mobile technology for Thomson Reuters. He acts as a mentor for Apps for Good projects and is very proud of his employers' commitment to the programme and increasing role – it already provides 17 mentors and will sponsor more awards.

'I love this programme,' he told those gathered for Apps for Good's London event.

> I feel we have poured our hearts and souls into it. We love the fact that kids get so excited about this stuff. Let me point out one thing that I hope every single one of you notices as you glance over here at this lovely crowd of people [the award-winning students]. Guess what you see – girls.

'Girls turn tech,' he announced to whoops and applause from the crowd. 'That absolutely thrills me because we have such a challenge in technology trying to get girls excited about tech.' More than half of the schools involved in Apps for Good are girls' schools.

> With such a large number of entries from across the UK, to have two winners not just from Scotland, but from a single school in the Highlands and Islands is particularly exciting. It shows that young people from anywhere, even the most remote location, can excel in this field and make a difference.

With a persona more Silicon Valley developer than corporate IT, Bob Schukai has the ruffled, urban cool of a David Duchovny character, a user-friendly interface to the immense industry experience and sharp business analysis that lie behind, gilded by reassuring personal charm. He's probably the only person that most of his London launch audience have seen wearing Google Glass. So he is a perfect bridge between the worlds he inhabits and is a popular mentor for students.

The eight years he spent in the UK did not prepare him, however, for his two visits to Wick High School. His directions were, broadly, go as far north as you can and then keep on going: 'Just when you think you can't get any further you get to Wick.' Not that he has to visit every school, as Apps for Good makes full use of electronic communications, including video conferencing.

In fact Bob Schukai is part of a revealing Apps for Good anecdote. 'One of my favourite stories was from one of my cadre schools, Westfield Primary,' said Debbie Forster, herself a former headteacher.

> They had a team of kids they had prepped. A few of the kids might even be kids who find classrooms challenging. The teacher is necessary here. The teacher got the kids ready to present to Bob online through Skype. They knew who Bob is and they were very daunted.

> When they gave him the app idea, he immediately said – he's magic, Bob; there is nothing he doesn't know about the field – 'Right, what you want to look at is . . . ' And he showed them an app that did these things. At which point the kids looked at him confidently, at the ripe age of ten or 11, and said, 'Thank you very much. We will take that idea under consideration.'

She laughed. 'They kept a straight face, and so did he, and, apparently, at the end of the phone call he was in hysterics and they were high-fiving. They understood that just because someone says something it doesn't necessarily mean that it's true.'

The role of the teacher is central in this work, and Apps for Good helps teachers open up their classrooms and their children to a much wider world of information. Debbie Forster said:

> It has been an interesting journey, because to some degree learning and education are always about information. But how and where do we get the information? The control of information changes, and who has to be in charge of the information to curate it and give it has changed. And I think the place we are in now, there is the idea that learning is universal.
>
> We are always going to be humans who learn from stories and connections etc. That does not change. But where information comes into that – who owns it, who accesses it – begins to become more fluid. It's a scary time. We have all listened to the talks, where education gets a little scared that everything is going to fall apart.
>
> We are in an interesting place of democratisation, and achieving quality versus quantity. I think within education it's really powerful. What we have seen with Apps for Good is teachers realising that mobile technology – the technology and the flow that comes through it – needn't be a threat.
>
> It can feel scary because there is so much out there. What's our role? What do we do? And it always comes down to control. How do I know? How am I in charge? How do I keep on top of that?

Debbie Forster's experience with technology has shown her that those concerns are a distraction, and teachers need to hold on to their confidence. She went on:

> I see the teachers that are coming to Apps for Good have the confidence to realise they are the pedagogical experts. They understand that this is the domain in which they need to make sure their expertise is razor sharp, and then the information becomes less important because that can be drawn on from elsewhere. That can be young people accessing information themselves but it can also be through technology. You can bring other experts, as it were virtually, into the classroom.

One of those virtual experts, Bob Schukai, explained:

> We couldn't do that before. Because I am US-based I can come and visit some of the schools maybe once or twice in a year. But for me to be able to interact with the number of schools that I do throughout the course of a school term I rely on video conferencing. So I will be using Skype or Google Hangouts or something like that. The kids see me; I can see them. We can easily share documents electronically so that I can have a look at what they are doing.

I am actually much better prepped when I meet with them because I am told ahead of time, 'This is the group, these are the kids, this is their idea, these are some of the questions they are already thinking about.' Quite a while ago, none of this capability really existed.

These virtual visits, along with the real ones, extend his role as a sponsor to one as a valuable, highly active curriculum resource.

He has no doubt about the importance of mobile technology for learning, although takes care to say that it shouldn't be used thoughtlessly, as a prop.

I think that when you look at the way education has changed what I have noticed first and foremost is how my own kids are using tech. At my son's school, where he started as a Year 6 student, he was given an iPad from day one and his classes and his homework are all delivered via the iPad. Now that he has moved into high school the iPad is used some but a lot of the work is focused on using a computer, with electronic delivery both for learning as well as for homework submissions.

Things like this are really, really useful for my son who is dyslexic. So just think about this classic struggle, and the high achievers who are dyslexic who were told they were dumb, they were stupid and they would never amount to anything. And imagine if these guys had had access to this kind of technology at a much younger age – that could have helped them read and learn much, much faster.

You wonder whether it would have done something different to the way their careers turned out quite honestly. I think that technology has an amazing way of revolutionising the way not only kids can learn but also interact – with other kids, with other teachers, with other cultures. It's tremendous to think what we can put on to our tablets and our phones because of the amount of memory that's on these things.

Some popular debates position the teacher as 'the guide on the side', as 'curators', but Debbie Forster sees the role as far more important than that. And that relationships lie at the heart of the work. 'Once the relationship is there you can help and draw in all the other bits and pieces,' she said.

So I think it's an exciting time; it's a tricky time but what we are understanding is that educators still have a central role. They can use technology to free them up to do what they do best and what they love most, which is the relationships with young people and getting the best from them.

Educators stay in the game and keep their pedagogy sharp to understand what technology can do, what it can't do, what its limitations are, what its benefits are, that it's another tool in our armoury. That means we have the best things for young people and draw on the whole wealth of information out there, and then again go back to what we do best – teaching young people how to problem-solve, teaching young people how to evaluate, to ask questions. It's no longer about making sure they have the right answer; it's helping them understand how they can best formulate the right question.

So the whole ethos that has developed in Apps for Good is that teachers are absolutely necessary, but in a different role and doing something that they can remain current on and can be the expert on, but they don't have to be the expert on everything. As Debbie Forster puts it:

I think that what is so exciting about this modern revolution is that it allows us new spaces for expertise. It's so hard sometimes when you are in front of kids and feeling, 'I have to know everything'. Particularly if you are a young teacher. That sense of 'Oh my God, what if one of them asks . . . and there is something I don't know'. I think technology frees us up to think 'I hope so', 'Of course, and if not we are going to find somebody who does. But I am the one to come to for questions. Not answers – questions'.

An analogy that Debbie Forster and her colleagues now use with their teachers for their changing roles is 'rock–climbing coach'. She explained:

Setting your young people free does not mean you've got an extra hour in the staffroom with a cup of tea. You're still there but you've got to do something that's a little uncomfortable. You stay on the ground. The young people are up climbing the mountain. They are going at different rates. Some are struggling and will have to come back down and renegotiate. You can't possibly know every handhold but you are still valuable.

You know if I am going to do rock climbing up a mountain I want the coach on the ground asking me questions, talking me through, helping me when I am panicking etc. Because of technology and what we do in Apps for Good we can bring in other experts. My teacher is the pedagogical expert, asking those questions to keep the children's confidence up. But then I can also, because of technology, be an expert there as well – maybe I am someone who does user interface, someone who is a project manager. I have sat in on these calls, and it's magic because the teacher is still there, helping kids understand and ask questions. The expert can answer but the kids then take it in a different direction.

Another important role for the teacher, and the school too, is ensuring that this work can find a place in the curriculum, rather than being something that doesn't fit, that can't properly be assessed. 'Here's the thing,' said Debbie Forster.

Here's the challenge. When I first went into the field this was very much extracurricular. We were on the edge and rebels. But I think there is a powerful moment in realising how many rebels there are out there.

Without us wanting to we have 75 per cent of our schools who are delivering this in the curriculum. So while we are saying that the best things don't happen in school, I get a lot of teachers who believe (and who are rebelling with us) that you can help it happen in school if you are willing to continue to disrupt. So yes, I have got now those valuable 'not school' things happening in the curriculum and that is because I do think that if you scratch the surface of teachers who work within an institution there are a lot of really constructive rebels there. We moved into it because we wanted to be different.

Every year we are serving our teachers and our kids, senior teachers etc. What they love is the kids talking about how important it is for them that the learning is about things that they choose, they own, they believe in, that it has a real-world context to see how it looks out into the outside world. But again, I would say I am over the moon. I am the last person to teacher-bash or school-bash. Heads have told me: 'Anything you want me to do?'

Apps for Good is a fitting title for a project that grew out of the favelas of Brazil where its 'parent' company, CDI, started running computer-based learning programmes in the 1990s. Anyone looking for evidence only has to look at this 2013 crop of award-winning students, with apps ranging from Puckupation (to generate jobs for pocket money) and Pitch Pals (for tuning stringed instruments) through Story Wall (to get more young people writing their stories) and Supportive Schedule (supporting independence for those with mental health issues) to the Wick winners and Social Bank (encouraging youngsters to set targets for their savings). Information about them (and the 2014 winners) is on the Apps for Good website.[6]

Apps for Good describes itself as an 'open-source technology education movement that aims to build a new global generation of problem solvers and makers: students who can create, launch and market new products that change the world'. It 'provides the course content, training and connections to expert volunteers, and then lets teachers do what they are best at – inspiring and guiding young people'. It works with students aged 10 to 18 years of age and, through its unique partnership approach to schools, balanced on a range of sponsors and expert volunteers, it appears to be well on its way to its goals.

The students appear to love it. Celebrating their success with Cattle Manager, Wick students John, Kieran and Ryan, commented:

The Apps for Good course gave us wonderful insight into the correct way to plan, structure and create effective apps ready to take to market. We strongly believe that our apps will have great demand. In terms of our future careers and lives this has been a unique opportunity. To win the award was the icing on the cake!

One thing is for sure, that this kind of work can give young people a more relevant, engaging and richer learning experience than simply following a rigid and narrow national curriculum is likely to provide. In fact, the possibility of being incorporated into such a curriculum would be anathema to Apps for Good, as Debbie Forster explained:

> I have no interest in someone announcing that every school will do Apps for Good. That would be the kiss of death for us. I don't want anyone 'having' to do Apps for Good, and we will sometimes spend as much time saying to a school, 'I don't think it's right for you yet, and here's another organisation that might work for you.' What I love is those schools that want to, that opt in, that want something different.

Notes

1 Apps for Good: http://www.appsforgood.org/ (accessed 28 July 2014).
2 Cattle Manager app: https://play.google.com/store/apps/details?id=com.catman (accessed 28 July 2014).
3 Dog Log: https://play.google.com/store/apps/details?id=com.afga.doglog (accessed 28 July 2014).
4 Novoda: http://novoda.com/ (accessed 28 July 2014).
5 Plant Pot: http://plantpot.co/ (accessed 28 July 2014).
6 Apps for Good 2013 award winners: www.appsforgood.org/public/student-apps (accessed 28 July 2014).

11 Two international perspectives

Familiar challenges – dissimilar situations

The situations that Andrew Rhodes and Miguel Nussbaum occupy are very different, diametrically opposed across the globe, yet the challenges they face echo across that space.

Andrew Rhodes is a British teacher working at the International School of Stavanger in Norway as director of technology – 'responsible for most things with a plug,' as he puts it. It is a fee-paying school of around 750 pupils from age three to 18 years, with 49 nationalities represented among the student body. These are children from prosperous families in a comparatively well-off country – whose citizens enjoy an average income of $55,400 (£32,927) per year, the 10th best in the world according to the CIA World Factbook[1] (www.cia.gov). Norwegian children stay at school until age 18, with 95 per cent of them attending some form of nursery provision, and 38 per cent of the 5.1 million population having a university education.

Chile, by comparison, is not so well off, either financially or educationally, achieving only 74th place on the personal prosperity scale, with an average income of $19,100 (£11,350), having an educational career lasting usually to age 15, with 42 per cent of its three-year-olds at nursery, and 29 per cent of its 17.3 million population attending university. Still, it has the best education results in Latin America, according to Organisation for Economic Co-operation and Development (OECD)[2] Programme for International Student Assessment (PISA) tests, designed to provide performance comparison information at state level. However, comparative success when measured against immediate neighbours is no reason for complacency for Professor Miguel Nussbaum from the Catholic University of Chile. As a member of the board of the National Agency for the Quality of Education he wants to bring about fundamental change to the education system, reshaping how teachers work and use resources in every school at every level.

Despite their different educational roles, in different hemispheres and with different starting points, they are both working to bring about systemic change in their particular situations, with technology as a primary driver. For Andrew Rhodes it is about moving a successful school on to embracing technology fully: having adopted a 1:1 programme using tablet computers (iPads), now he wants to change what happens in every classroom. As does Miguel Nussbaum, only on a much larger scale.

'Over 60 per cent of our children, especially in the public schools, don't get minimum standards after eight years of basic schooling,' Miguel Nussbaum explains as he outlines Chile's education crisis. 'They are incapable of solving arithmetic problems or of understanding what they are reading.'

It is an 'extremely exhaustive' curriculum, the result of which is that students don't learn the necessary content before they are moved on to the next step, gradually getting further and further behind in their studies. 'So after eight years they don't learn anything; we are cheating society,' he states. In his view young people leave school ill prepared to play their part in society.

However, he believes that the issue is not just the content of the curriculum but also how children are taught, that teachers are not well prepared for the classroom by universities, and not well supported once in post. The first part of this dilemma, he suggests, can be addressed by teaching critical thinking.

> The world is formed of data but not of questions, so we have to learn to pose questions. And once we have those questions know how to solve those questions and compare if the results really are consistent with the world that we are observing. For me critical thinking is the key.

This doesn't mean that curriculum content has no place, but that to prepare the next generation to meet the 'threats and needs of the next 20 years' requires abilities that currently are not taught in schools.

Alongside shifting the emphasis from content, Miguel Nussbaum also wants to see improvements in the use of resources, the development of an 'orchestrated' approach, the integration of conventional and digital resources.

> Orchestration is basically the best practices. How do we use, in the best possible way, the time inside the classroom? It is not about technology. How do we integrate paper-based activities, *PowerPoint* activities, interactive activities, collaborative activities?

Within this process he sees developing the use of technology as having its own particular difficulties, with two initial, identifiable stages where resistance occurs. It is, he believes, rather like getting a new phone. For the first couple of hours, or even days, there is a level of frustration that we encounter that tempts us simply to throw it away and go back to our old one. However, if we persevere we learn to manage the new device, even if we don't necessarily get to like it, perhaps believing that the previous one was easier to operate.

'What happens with teachers and the critical change is exactly the same,' he says.

> At the beginning it only gets worse. 'This is horrible. I'm going to have 30 or 40 kids in front of me,' so you need to support the teacher. The second critical phase is 'Yeah, I manage the technology but the way I did it before

was much easier and less cumbersome than the system now.' So there you also have to support the teachers. We support the teachers only with initial teacher training. With these two critical phases we do not.

Andrew Rhodes' route to introducing the use of technology in his school was perhaps a little more straightforward, although there are parallels in bringing about widespread acceptance of its role. When he first started at the school in autumn 2010 there was one PC in each classroom, a couple of computer suites and 'two or three laptop trolleys' which 'weren't being used' and 'didn't really work'. He instigated something of a technological renaissance, bringing in 350 iMacs (desktops) and MacBooks (laptops), 60–70 of which are spread out across the school in different subject areas. Staff have a laptop and an iPad. But the biggest change was instigating a 1:1 programme for students.

They chose iPads for all students for a number of reasons, in part because they all had access to more conventional technology – desktops or laptops – at home, and to a large degree when needed at school. Then there is the convenience:

> If you want to do 30 seconds' research in a lesson it does not take much longer than 30 seconds. With laptops you have to get the laptops out, then deal with the kids that forgot their passwords. That 30 seconds' research takes a lot longer than 30 seconds.

But the main reason is that, says Andrew Rhodes, 'The iPad has the best eco-system out there for supporting learning.' Apps have been tested so are very unlikely to affect the device negatively and cause it to malfunction, and users can largely manage them themselves, downloading apps for free, or very cheaply, without needing the intervention of technical support staff.

The result of introducing this critical mass of technology to the International School in Stavanger has been the kind of changes in practice that Miguel Nussbaum seeks in Chile, but with the pressure for such a shift not coming from above, from the Ministry of Education or the teacher training institutions, but from the students themselves. Andrew Rhodes explains:

> In terms of practicalities in the classroom it changes the dynamic in the classroom instantly. The students have these devices and they expect to be using them in lessons. They expect the teacher to be expert with the technology very quickly.

Regardless of where the impetus for a shift in classroom activity comes from, though, the stages of implementation remain the same:

> When we started our one-to-one, when we gave out 500 or so iPads, there was me. Everything came to me. I went from supporting just the teachers to suddenly being tech support as well for 500 or so pupils who had just got an iPad.

He came up with an innovative solution. As a school that teaches the International Baccalaureate (IB), older students are required to undertake an element of community service. For some of the boys – many conforming to social stereotypes of a particular interest in computers correlating with social awkwardness – this flood of technology provided an opportunity to be of particular use, and to raise their social cachet. 'Two weeks ago a student arrived from Russia,' he adds. 'Within 24 hours of being at school he's got an iPad, we've set up a school email, we've given him an iTunes card, and so you need someone to help them get their heads around: "This is what your English teacher is using it for, this is how your science teacher is using it".'

With this rudimentary level of technical support in place he could then focus on the more important question for staff of how to use the iPads in teaching and learning. He explains:

> The support requests we are now getting a lot of at school are, 'I want to do this on the iPads – How would I do it and what apps would I use?' They are conversations about teaching often, or they can *become* conversations about teaching. They might start off as conversations about apps, but we can kind of mould them into conversations about teaching.

As an example of the kind of teaching activity that has now become possible, Andrew Rhodes tells a sixth-form maths lesson. 'I was in an IB maths class where the teacher had shared maths problems using Showbie [a sharing app],' he says. 'Rather than just record the answers in Notability [to record notes], just go into Explain Everything, hit record and explain to me the process that you are going through as you are working through these problems.' With this app students are able to talk over the screen content, whatever format it is in, and add notations to illustrate points. Once complete, the teacher could share each solution on the interactive whiteboard, with the real-time commentary recorded as the students worked through the problem. This led into a discussion that allowed each of them to reflect on their solution, and to hear ideas from others, stopping and starting the recording as necessary to pull out discussion points.

It is the kind of class interaction, critical thinking perhaps, that Miguel Nussbaum is working towards in Chile. For some years he has been developing a system for improving collaboration and the development of social communication skills in classrooms, known as Eduinnova.[3] The pupils are randomly allocated to a small group, then the whole class is posed a question. Each group has to come to a unanimous response before sharing it with the rest of the class. For instance, 'What would be the greatest benefit of persuading all children to walk to school?' The suggestions from each group would then be shared with the whole class, choices made about the best ideas, followed by further debate on those until further sharing and eventually consensus is reached. By using handheld technology ideas can be shared easily both within and across groups. The latest iteration requires group members to record an argument to support their particular position, and to take on specific roles in order to bring about meaningful collaboration. In order to make a sound case learners have to ensure they have a proper understanding of the content of the lesson.

Having a distinct position within the group is also key.

> The other thing that we are working on in the Eduinnova model is the role. There have to be roles. It is very important when you do collaboration that there are clear roles between the peers so that each of them has a task which is independent of the others. So there is a clear interdependence between the members of the group.

However, taking this approach to developing critical thinking skills is not without difficulties. 'One of the biggest problems we have today is that teachers have a confusion between cooperation and collaboration,' Miguel Nussbaum explains. 'In cooperation what happens is you divide the task in parts and afterwards you put the parts together. In collaboration there is a clear interdependence between the roles of the kids.'

It is, he believes, the emergence of technology as a classroom tool, particularly handheld devices, that makes this kind of activity possible. 'I am completely convinced that without technology you cannot teach collaboration.' However, it is not the only prerequisite for success.

> I would say that tablets and mobiles have a beautiful infrastructure for teaching critical thinking and collaboration. However, for reaching that you have to have the adequate software on one side, and on the other the teacher has to know how to make use of those resources inside the classroom. So it is not about the technology, it is about the software and how the teacher uses those resources inside the classroom.

The approach Miguel Nussbaum and his team are taking to equipping the teachers is a very prescriptive one.

> We have to guide them and show them how to manage the different resources that are available, to use their time and their resources in the best possible way. That means the teacher has to follow the script in a strict way but it means that you guide the teacher in a new role. So he sees how to really transform his practices.

If the teacher adheres strictly to the brief then change will occur, rather like 'opening a new door which they haven't seen before so we have to show them at least the beginning of what it looks like inside'.

Without this very strict guidance, his belief is the benefits in both approach and equipment will not be realised, as has happened before. 'The problem is, if you see what we have done before, especially with interactive whiteboards, we just automised and technologised the old classroom – but we didn't change the classroom.'

In Stavanger Andrew Rhodes' approach to implementation in the classroom was less rigid, giving the staff carte blanche to use what they wanted, and in the way they saw fit – initially at least.

> When we deployed we gave teachers free choices about how they did things – for me choice is a good thing. With things like sharing work, for example, there is email, there are Dropbox and Onedrive, there is Showbie, and things now that teachers are using like Schoology.

While remaining an advocate of teachers making their own decisions about the best way to work in their classroom, he realised that this wasn't always the best thing for the learners.

> From the students' point of view they might be getting nine different ways for sharing a file when they are first getting to grips with the technology and using it for learning. Having a way of sharing in maths, a different way of sharing in English, and another way of sharing in science – and the French teacher just says email it to her.

This resulted in a situation where staff were finding that they each had to teach their own preferred method of handing in work, whereas if they all used the same app they would be reinforcing each other's teaching. 'So we have gone from, "You can do whatever you want", to, "Actually we would like you to use these two or three different ways of doing things – at least to start with".'

It was a freedom that staff were not all comfortable with either, many preferring a more directed approach. 'Not very many of my teachers will see half an hour of their teaching prep time as being well spent if they have gone on the app store and found a whole load of new apps,' he explains.

While Andrew Rhodes was working on developing a 'meaningful workflow' (bringing together a number of apps in one activity to create a final outcome), he believes that 'most teachers still are not at the point where they are prepared to sit and spend the time it takes to work out how to do it well. They want someone to do that bit for them.'

It could be that the teachers are somewhat daunted by the task of sifting and sorting all that is available. 'There is so much software and so much digital content, but the problem is this software and this digital content are not necessarily quality contents,' points out Miguel Nussbaum.

> It's like a book – not all the books are worthwhile and software is the same. So before you use it you have to know it is really worthwhile, and that means you have to spend time studying the software to see if it is really the quality you are looking for.

In Stavanger Andrew Rhodes thinks one answer is for teachers to create their own teaching materials. 'We have teachers using PowerPoint and Smart Notebook

– very easy to convert into useful presentations.' Once created, content can be sent to students through iTunes U, a facility designed for just such a purpose. An advantage of which is that it is

> using a lot of the powers of mobile technology, it is pushing notifications to the device to say, 'Mr Rhodes has updated his course', or, 'This is the new deadline for that piece of work'. You are starting to use mobile devices for things they are really good at.

One problem that both men identify is that the need for investment goes beyond funding the technology into developing ways of using it. As Miguel Nussbaum puts it, 'Everybody is buying tablets and nothing is changing'. Andrew Rhodes agrees:

> There aren't many people who can't use an iPad, but there are an awful lot of schools and teachers who need a hell of a lot of support because they have gone out and brought a load of iPads and don't understand philosophically how to get it to work in their school.

Even with a lot of support for schools it can be difficult to bring about long lasting effects.

As an academic, Miguel Nussbaum has long been testing out ideas in schools and examining the impact, although not always with the long-term outcomes he might want.

> To our knowledge nobody has really reached the capacity of transferring those practices in such a way that they maintain for a couple of years. Once the researchers go out the practices go out.

However he remains optimistic: 'What we are doing is showing the way, and we do hope in ten years something will happen. Society is demanding it.'

While the research has been successful, what he wants to achieve is transformation of a whole system.

> I would say that we have shown on a small scale that technology can make real improvements in learning and in the development of social abilities, but I would say I haven't seen it at a state level. That means 50,000 kids, 100,000 kids, those improvements.

In fact currently the evidence he has is that introducing computers into schools can have the opposite effect.

> The Chilean government has made a huge investment – hundreds of millions of dollars – in the last 20 years, and today the public schools have a ratio of nine kids for one computer, which is quite high. We made a study last year of

the correlation between the use of the technology and the improvement in the national pace of improvement in mathematics and what we discovered is there is a relatively high correlation of 0.59. But that correlation is negative. That means that the more they use technology, the less is the improvement in the national tests in maths of eighth-grade students.

He doesn't see this as an indictment of the technology, but of the skills of the teachers in using it.

Andrew Rhodes also thinks that it is not possible to disentangle the technology from the teaching in order to investigate any changes in pupil outcomes. 'If you are integrating it in the right way in the classroom it is difficult to say quantitatively the impact it is having on learning,' he thinks.

> One of the reasons we have seen big impacts in parts of the school is because of the teachers and the way they have embraced it. To say, 'The iPads have made two grades difference in English,' is to take away all the work that that teacher has done to integrate the technology to the point that it becomes invisible.

Although 'with technology, as it gets easier to use, teachers seem to be needing more and more support to integrate it into the classroom'.

However, for both of them the challenge remains to get 100 per cent take-up of not just new technologies, but also of ways of teaching in their respective systems. As Andrew Rhodes puts it:

> There are still some attitudes that need to change a bit. I try and focus on 80 per cent doing great stuff rather than the 20 per cent that aren't. But there does come a point − and we are starting to get to that point − where there are some things that need to happen at a management level to positively encourage the last 20 per cent, and that is a challenge because that does need an attitude change.

In part it is down to the academic success of the school.

> There is still this mismatch with particularly high school and secondary education where because you have exam classes you are judged on the quality of your results. Sometimes a teacher is not doing transformation but still somehow got great results − mainly because the kids would have got great results anyway − just by giving them the textbooks and the worksheets. A change of attitude needs to happen there.

There is a similar concern in Chile. However, it is not one based on entrenched success, but on a missed opportunity, as Miguel Nussbaum puts it: 'What I am worried about is that with all that technology, if it is not used adequately, not only that we won't improve learning, but our measures show that it will diminish learning.'

Notes

1 The CIA World Factbook is an expansive body of international data that is collected from a variety of US Government agencies and hundreds of published sources. It is presented on The World Factbook website which is updated every week (www.cia.gov) (accessed 30 April 2014).

2 The Organisation for Economic Co-operation and Development (OECD) works with governments to understand what drives economic, social and environmental change. It measures productivity and global flows of trade and investment and analyses and compares data to predict future trends. It is also responsible for setting international standards on a wide range of things, from agriculture and tax to the safety of chemicals.

3 Eduinnova: www.theguardian.com/education/2007/jun/19/elearning.technology9 (accessed 30 April 2014).

PART

III

The analysis

12

Expert views

> *Q: How many psychotherapists does it take to change a light bulb?*
>
> *A: That all depends. They have to want to change first.*

Can mobile technologies change learning and teaching? On their own probably not, but experts in the field who were polled for this book broadly agree that they are a powerful tool for change for those schools, educators and learners wanting to transform learning.

Of course there is a wide range of opinion and excitement, and even those who feel that learning itself has not changed believe that rich aspects of teaching and learning are changing with the technology. For example, before the emergence of ubiquitous technologies, flipped learning didn't have the profile it currently enjoys.

Most common were constructive blends of positive and negative, like education consultant Dewi Lloyd,[1] who commented:

> I don't think that the process of learning is changing; it's the relevance and authenticity of the activities, the quality of the outcomes and the size of the audience that's different. It has the potential to change the mechanics of teaching from the perspective of schooling.

> I became interested in mobile learning as a way of ensuring that the valuable face to face time in lessons was used far more for discussion and review as opposed to a place where the 'work' was created. Few schools have radically transformed the timetable allowing more freedom and independence for students to lead their own projects and call on subject specialists as and when they need them.

In what's commonly known as flipped learning, children tend to research concepts via online materials out of class and then use class time to explore them further with their teacher and peers. Traditional classwork and homework activities are reversed, so teachers focus on application of knowledge rather than acquisition.

One of the most positive respondents was Dan Buckley,[2] deputy headteacher of Saltash.net Community College,[3] a fellow of Education Impact and the creator of

Personalisation by Pieces.[4] Can mobile technology help bring about change? 'Yes, absolutely, as fast as we will allow it to,' he said.

> The impact which it has is determined by the ways students are allowed to use it. There is evidence that if used didactically for individualised learning involving just student and device then this can have a negative impact. Alternatively, if used in environments involving choice and ownership by learners then the diversity expands and creative problem solving begins.

The research, he said, points to student-centred learning being the ideal fit for mobile and handheld. 'Individualised learning, doesn't,' he warned, 'although this is the kind of use that most schools mistakenly try to use it for.

> In 2000–2004 I did an implementation of 1:1 which resulted in the school jumping to top 20 in the country in terms of achievement. Over the next two years we used it to accelerate schools from failing to outstanding rapidly. I am currently looking at how you implement non-disruptively and we have had reports of progress in terms of achievement in under two months.

> In my former role as international director of research [for Cambridge Education],[5] I had to do countless repeats of comparing research evidence in support of these two extremes of the pedagogical spectrum. There is so much research evidence in favour of student-centred learning, and so much evidence that individualised can be harmful, that it is remarkable the debate is still raging on.

If anyone should know about mobile technology and changing learning it's Essa Academy director Abdul Chohan, who has been at the forefront of change for a number of years. He is understandably upbeat. 'Mobile technology is creating a paradigm shift for learning,' he said.

> For a long time educators have been very good at doing the wrong things really well. Asking the 'Why' question has enabled shift to happen. This has meant investment in mobile technology rather than traditional laptop trolley/computer room infrastructure.

> For the first time, students have had 24-hour access to learning. The ability to ask the right questions is a key skill. Mobile technology allows two-way access for the learner. Students can ask questions as they get inspired by experiences. Traditionally, students would have to wait until they came back to school or logged in to a desktop/laptop computer.

> Globalisation of economy means that increasingly students of diverse cultures and languages are seen in schools. Mobile technology becomes the digital pencil case that students tap into in order to access a variety of tools that are personalised for their needs.

Impact on learning has been very evident. We have seen an increase in results in a remarkably short time. Additionally, we have seen a growth in the social capital of students as they become confident learners that are ready for a world that doesn't exist yet.

There is a sense of frustration however, even among those who have already tasted success with handheld projects. Consultant Dave Whyley,[6] who led Wolverhampton's successful Learning2Go project,[7] said:

Unfortunately, with the demise of Becta[8] and other national bodies the same mistakes are being made by schools with their mobile learning implementations. There is plenty of past documentation and research but it is not being either made visible or being heeded.

Throughout the development of mobile learning, from its outset to today's fashionable interactive devices, the critical issues have remained the same for anyone embarking on the mobile learning journey. Among these are learner choice, adapting curriculum planning, assessment, teacher professional development and maintaining equity.

Although he was broadly positive about mobile technology, he warned:

Mobile technology can change teaching and learning but only if it is part of a deeper vision for the way in which children learn within an educational establishment. Implemented badly, without a clear vision of the objectives, it will fail and actually could have a negative effect.

Dewi Lloyd also worked on the Learning2Go project. He agreed about the potential benefits. 'Mobile devices can hold the key to rich project-based learning,' he said, adding: '"How can I facilitate high-quality design process, problem solving and critical thinking?" should be the starting point, not "Which device should we choose?"'

He lamented the slowness in learning lessons from developments so far:

I think that the key for me is that little innovation in the ICT camp has filtered through to those leaders who have responsibility for teaching and learning. A good example of this is in the way these devices are used for assessment. I could have a richer picture of my students' understanding throughout the lesson than has ever been possible and yet few have taken advantage of this.

Sadly I see many 1:1 classrooms where we could replace the devices with a few typewriters, cameras and encyclopaedias!

Civil servant Vanessa Pittard,[9] who formerly held a brief for research at the now-defunct government ICT agency Becta, and later for ICT at the Department for Education (DfE),[10] is cautiously positive about change. Asked whether mobile technologies can change teaching and learning, she replied:

The answer is yes, though the evidence we have picks up indicators rather than direct evidence of changes to learning. We no longer survey schools directly, but we take note of evidence from BESA [British Educational Suppliers Association][11] and other sources, which has recently shown:

- a growth in the proportion of PCs that are now tablets in schools, and strong indications that schools intend to purchase larger numbers of tablet devices;

- innovative schools adopting 1–1 tablet schemes (see Tablets for Schools project);[12]

- strong recognition from industry that the shift from desktops/laptops to tablet availability is important for education;

- large numbers of educational apps (a developer recently told us that there are around 2,000 maths learning apps in the market). Most of them are not pedagogically informed however.

In her ICT role at the DfE she had noted the increased role of mobile technologies and visited 1:1 schools where there was 'more evidence of real-time student research in class and a more questioning style of teaching linked to that'.

Vanessa Pittard also warned that priorities should be the right way around:

I think we need to be cautious when experimenting with pedagogy. We shouldn't let the technology lead the pedagogy. A sound evidence base is essential, and I welcome the work of, for example, Nesta,[13] the Education Endowment Foundation[14] and the Nominet Trust,[15] as well as the CSR [corporate social responsibility] contributions of commercial organisations (e.g. the Tablets for Schools not-for-profit project) in committing to research in this area.

One person deeply involved in research into mobile technology for learning, and over a significant period of time, is Elizabeth Hartnell-Young, who is director of the Australian Council for Educational Research (ACER) Institute[16] and is also well known for her work in this area with the University of Nottingham's Learning Sciences Research Institute (LSRI).[17] 'I like to think of mobile and fixed technologies as part of a rich provision of interacting technologies,' she explained.

In the Victorian Department of Education and Early Childhood Development (DEECD),[18] about 650 students from 32 primary and secondary schools participated in a research project from 2009–12 (DEECD, 2012).[19]

Technologies used included digital cameras, voice recorders, iPods, tablets, netbooks, animation and gaming software and interactive whiteboards. Most tasks required more than one technology. Evidence was collected through formal assessments, teachers' observations, surveys, focus groups and interviews and showed that what was important in engaging students and improving their learning included:

- students taking responsibility for the pace of their learning, and choosing resources to suit their learning styles and levels of prior knowledge

- enabling students to work beyond the classroom walls and school hours, drawing on their personal networks and experiences

- continual feedback between students, teachers and peers, and opportunities for reflection, through blogs, wikis and especially student-created films and podcasts

- students working in teams and taking roles as leaders, negotiators and resource managers.

Elizabeth Hartnell-Young said that teachers' most important role was in 'teaching students how to learn', and this changed relationships.

> Mobile technology is changing power relations in learning, as students now have access to as much information as their teachers in a 'just in time' way, so that the challenge for teachers is to guide students to make critical judgements about the value of information. The constant production of material, apps and devices by technology companies, and the aggressive moves of these companies into education means that there is also a danger that consumption will trump creation.

This danger meant that 'with "byte-size" information, fragmentation could overtake coherence, and ephemera may overtake history,' she warned. 'That's why places to store personal information are important. On the positive side, mobile technology is also enabling semiotic democracy (Fiske) where students remix and repost.'

At the heart of the teacher–learner relationship is understanding. A fundamental for teachers is to know their learners. The better they know them the easier it is to support them and to personalise the learning. 'Through mobile technologies it is possible to know our students better,' said Elizabeth Hartnell-Young.

> Research with indigenous students in the Northern Territory of Australia showed that they were able to use mobile devices to capture aspects of their culture to share with their teachers, who were able to use this material as authentic curriculum input. This enhanced the relationship between teachers and students, and gave rich material for literacy learning.[20]

This change in relationships is also something highlighted by Carol Allen,[21] school improvement adviser for ICT and inclusion in North Tyneside. 'I feel the opportunity for the student as creator is the greatest strength emerging, whether it is by creating digital content or indeed coding applications for others to utilise,' she said. 'Capturing student voice has never been so relevant as it is today and, equally, not doing so is highlighted as a real weakness.'

Confirming that she thought mobile technologies were helping change learning, she said they were creating 'a sea change, offering immediacy, flexibility and personalisation, especially for learners with additional needs'.

'The ability to use devices to gather information, to research, check, collaborate and share forwards in any situation is incredibly powerful for all ages and stages of education.'

However, she acknowledges that even the most traditional drill and practice type of activity can be more effective with a change in the medium of delivery.

> It is interesting that many areas of education and approach have been enhanced by mobile technologies. Initially, attention is drawn to exciting and innovative work such as the student as content creator, or composer or collaborator and yet simple apps that consolidate and generalise basic skills learning, for example, times tables or spelling, are proving not only engaging and motivating but to be producing noticeable improvement in results (for example, Dawn Hallybone's work on handheld DS and spelling results) [see Chapter 5].

Dewi Lloyd agrees:

> Let's not, however, underestimate the power of these devices to engage the disaffected with even the most vanilla applications such as ebooks etc. Very often it's the difficulties of producing readable work that is the barrier to their success, so for them the simple act of writing is transformed (not very pedagogically advanced however).

The support that handheld technologies can provide to those who struggle to create text-based work is just one of the ways in which they are used for children and young people with special educational needs. As Carol Allen, a specialist in this field, points out:

> In the field of AAC [augmentative and alternative communication], the ability to have apps that allow speech generation on a small, handheld device has offered a much greater freedom for some users. For some the best solution will still be the more powerful, complex communication aids; however, for many 'light' users, a device in their pocket is sufficient and socially more acceptable.

> Currently, I am looking at how mobile technology can unlock the power of 'anytime anywhere' learning; the implications for both home/school collaboration and educational visits are immense if access to mobile technology is utilised with careful attention to pedagogical purpose rather than just using it because it is new and/or trendy.

Special needs and inclusion has also been an area of interest for Elizabeth Hartnell-Young. 'Mobile technologies for special needs offer hope for all students, including the growing proportion of elderly,' she pointed out.

> If we are really serious about personalising learning we need to look at the small-scale technology production and take opportunities to scale it up, making it more affordable.

At the Royal Children's Hospital in Melbourne, teachers work with families to keep patients connected to learning while they are in hospital. As well as the ubiquitous iPads, access to the learning platform, and video conferencing, some children and their teachers back at school use the Absent Classmate, an innovative technology that was developed at the hospital in conjunction with researchers from the University of Melbourne.

Based on an ambient orb (McCullough, 2005) it enables a child in any remote location to change the color of a glowing 'orb' or sphere in a distant classroom, by commanding it over the internet from a laptop. When the orb lights up or changes color, the teachers and students are reminded of their absent classmate. The orbs help children absent from school due to hospitalization to create a 'presence' for themselves in their class (Green, Vetere, Nisselle, Dang, Deng & Strong, 2011).[22]

While there was certainly general positivity among experts, the responses varied and there was caution. For example, Jocelyn Wishart,[23] senior lecturer in education at the Graduate School of Education, University of Bristol, could see changes and benefits at certain levels but not a change in learning.

'Mobile technology is changing the ways and modes in which learners communicate with their peers, access stored knowledge and also the range of the places where they have the opportunity to do this,' she said. 'It is extending the range of teaching opportunities, particularly ones linked to authentic settings available to lecturers and teachers. However, I wouldn't say that this was changing learning itself.'

One area of effectiveness that she identified, and her words were echoed by other experts, is where mobile technologies supported more authentic tasks for learning and teaching.

'Examples of pedagogical approaches that have been particularly enhanced are those that rely on students bringing information from authentic locations, or even accessing it in the field, to the classroom,' she explained.

I am thinking of Saku Ekanayake's PhD study where secondary school science teachers built images captured from home and the school garden into their teaching and of Gary Priestnall's work on augmenting landscapes in the Lake District so university students could overlay the geological processes upon the current scene.

I would also describe the use of students' own handhelds for instant feedback by classroom response systems such as Stuart Billington's easyvote (www. easyvote.co.uk/) as enhancing formative assessment opportunities. Drill and practice style pedagogical approaches are often presented as mobile learning; however, I wouldn't describe them as such, more as simple 'flashcard' style revision techniques.

In my own field, teaching education by promoting reflection on educational practice, the use of a digital or mobile phone camera to capture instances to support later reflection should work well but doesn't, as schoolwide bans on mobile technology use affect how confident teacher trainees are to use handheld devices in classroom contexts.

'Education practice itself has to change if some of the benefits of mobile devices are to be realised,' she said, pointing out that there should be greater acceptance of the use of 'video snapshots in supporting reflection'. This would require changed policies and practice in schools.

The slowness of change in assessment was also cited as a serious obstacle to progress. Dewi Lloyd said simply: 'The examination industry has no idea how to harness this power and is being left behind.'

Recognising learners' digital contributions was also a cause of concern for Dave Whyley. 'Acceptance of digital work is the "glass ceiling" for the ubiquitous use of mobile devices,' he added. 'As long as learners are not able to use technology to complete coursework and examinations there will be an "unnatural" block on its use on a day-to-day basis.'

> There have been interesting developments such as the e-Scape project[24] which have sought to address this. With the increased use of learning platforms' trackable storage then teachers might have some confidence that work completed by students may be visible and accessible for the usual accountability measures.

There was still a need for attitudes in schools to change, added Jocelyn Wishart:

> A wholesale change of culture is needed. We teach students in primary schools about road safety and in secondary schools to be responsible for safe sexual behaviour, so why haven't we yet invested similar levels of effort teaching responsible smartphone use?

Professor Stephen Heppell[25] pointed out that he first worked with mobile phones and learners back in the early 1990s, and although many schools were now more open to the idea there was still a problem.

> The concern here is for the schools that are still banning and blocking. They are getting left behind. For the adopters, there is perhaps not enough globally shared project activity, and not enough harnessing of the GPS capabilities (global positioning system). Perhaps two underdeveloped areas yet are 'big data' (a learner's dashboard on their own performance) and data capture.

There was still a lot to be discovered, he said, giving the example of a school he was working with in Italy where the students used internet access on their own mobile phones for the learning, 'and forgetting the school [computer] network other than for administration, with significant costs savings'.

However, he felt that mobile technologies had already changed learning:

> from changing the paradigm of institutional provision to transforming copying ('take a picture of the board and save it'). It has taken a flippin' long time for

the potential to be realised. I don't think kids will be this patient with the next emerging technology.

Dave Whyley also sees the success, or otherwise, of handheld learning in school being largely due to institutional reasons rather than the capabilities of the students.

Pedagogical approaches that have not worked have been all related to the devices being used without enough teacher training or a change in the pedagogical methods. Also by and large where the devices are owned by the school and are not taken home then the impact is restricted.

Dr Christina Preston,[26] who founded the Mirandanet international community of practice, was more circumspect, although convinced of the potential. 'I have evidence from bring your own device/technology (BYOD/BYOT) research in three schools that these kinds of device can be transformative,' she said, 'but only if they are part of a strategic plan to change pedagogy that is well prepared by the ICT coordinator with the support of the senior management team and with targeted pedagogical CPD [continuing professional development] for the staff.

Just buying them and having them around does nothing – I know one primary school where all the iPads are kept in a cupboard and got out for 30 minutes a day.

It is a view that is supported by consultant Mal Lee,[27] quoting a 2005 report.[28]

UNESCO warns that simply making technology equally available to all within a society will not suffice to bridge any knowledge divide that exists, since 'access to useful, relevant knowledge is more than simply a matter of infrastructure – it depends on training, cognitive skills and regulatory frameworks geared towards contents'.

Equity is also a concern where BYOT is pursued. Elizabeth Hartnell-Young points out that '"Bring your own device" policies can give students constant access, but can entrench inequities.'

Dave Whyley explains further:

This is a major concern. One of the reasons that UK schools opt for school uniforms is to make sure that no children are disadvantaged or bullied by the 'fashion show' syndrome. Imagine only being able to afford a hand-me-down Windows XP laptop and sitting next to a 'friend' who had the latest iPad?

Mal Lee, who researches and documents the evolution of schooling and teaching, is currently working on *Digital Normalisation and School Transformation* – *examining the impact that digital normalisation in and out of the school is having upon the nature of schooling.*

He is looking at the work of a cross-section of schools in the UK, USA, New Zealand and Australia that have reached the stage in their evolution where the school's total community – its staff, students and parents – 'have normalised the 24/7/365 use of their own, ever-evolving suite of digital technology in every facet of their lives, work and education and noting the impact that normalisation has upon every area of the school's operations, educational and administrative'.

He warned:

> It needs to be stressed that one is talking of an as yet small cadre of schools globally, and that while the young, their parents and society in general have all normalised the use of the digital, the vast majority of schools lag well behind.

The purpose of the work is to share the insights of the 'normalised' schools – which might have taken 15–20 years on their development journeys – to help those that want to catch up. Their journeys had much in common and the research identified approaching 50 key variables. One of them was 'the astute use of mobile technology, but as Professor Steve Higgins notes in his 2012 study of the impact of the digital on learning,[29] the kit alone will never enhance learning'.

He added, 'The impact on learning in the pathfinders comes from the school's creation of tightly integrated learning ecology focused on the realisation of the desired educational benefits.'

Mal Lee's interest in mobile technology was in the BYOT approach, where everyone is already familiar with their devices, which obviates the need for training in that area. He was also reluctant to tie the use of mobile technologies to particular pedagogies, preferring the more holistic model with its integrated key factors.

'What is emerging very strongly in my research is the whole of school pedagogy is one of the last areas to change,' he stressed, 'and that it is not until schools reach digital normalisation will the pedagogy fundamentally change.'

In this picture one of the key factors is trust, and a shift to placing the learner at the centre, as he explained:

> In relation to the possibilities for further change the challenge is not the 'gear' but rather the educator's mindset, the willingness to move from the current position of mistrust in the young and the imperative of the professional educators unilaterally controlling the teaching, learning and assessment process behind closed school walls to a position where they are prepared to trust the young, to genuinely collaborate with the homes and distribute control of the teaching among all the teachers of the young from birth onwards.

> The pathfinders are operating within the latter mode – where anything is possible. The vast majority of schools and governments are still in the control over mode and have years to travel on the evolutionary scale before they'll countenance any real change, such as allowing the kids to choose their own kit.

> The history of the use of instructional technology for near on a century has been characterised by distrust – distrust in the kids and indeed most teachers.

The astute use of the student's own ever-evolving suite of digital technology kit requires the school to do an about-face and work from a position of trust and respect – for the teachers, the students and the parents – and to allow the young to choose the hardware and software they believe most appropriate.

Despite the numerous caveats among the experts, however, there was no shortage of detailed, practical advice for implementing the adoption of mobile devices in schools. Dave Whyley was more than happy to share what he and colleagues had learned from Learning2Go. At the heart of any 1:1 or BYOD scheme, he said, there should be equity principles which are also supported by a common platform for communication and resources. In fact he created his own five-stage developmental model:

> In order to put the development of mobile learning into a pedagogical perspective I came up with this five-stage developmental model to begin to measure the impact of mobile technology implementations.
>
> 1. Low learner participation – receiving texts, messaging;
> 2. Learners as consumers – receiving content, podcasts, multimedia;
> 3. Learners as emergent creators – receiving rich content but with few tools to create;
> 4. Learners as fluent creators – sophisticated content and mobile creation tools to construct learning for review;
> 5. Integrated learners – as above but with a high level of integration with existing systems.

While our poll of educators stimulated a range of opinions and levels of optimism, the nearer the contributors were to successful projects, the stronger the belief in the potential for change.

Abdul Chohan feels that schools have to look at the bigger picture, but with learning at its heart. 'A holistic view of learning needs to be taken into consideration by school leaders,' he said. 'Doing the wrong things really well comes to mind when school leaders think about technology. Typically, a budget is set aside for technology and old equipment is replaced by new.

> Schools must look at technology from a learning and operational perspective. As I have discovered, this approach will lead to hidden operational benefits. Reduced costs for photocopying, textbooks, interactive whiteboards are just a few of the areas in which quite dramatic savings can be made.

Carol Allen echoed his views.

> An understanding by educators that technology is a tool, not an end in itself, thus purely by purchasing a mobile device for all of Year 7 will not effect the

desired change. By working out when mobile devices will be most useful; what functions suit each task; quality control over apps; whether devices are needed 1:1 or in groups with a single device and combining effective planning with a flexibility allowing creativity and freedom, there can be a sea change in potential!

There is an abundance of apps; they are spreading; they are self-seeding; reproducing exponentially, which means both that there are many dreadful apps and equally enough choice of good ones to allow for progression, differentiation and personalisation, but only if the educator has some strategy for choosing and applying to learning stages.

The last words have to go to Dan Buckley, whose passion for creative, collaborative learning is fuelled by years of research and the experience of working with schools, education authorities and governments across the globe. The last person to be dazzled by technology, or throw devices at a problem, he is fascinated by the way implementations like 1:1 schemes have the potential to unlock power relations that hold back learning. He looks forward to 'community cohesion through mixing mentors from the community and students of different ages ... We have multigenerational projects in which students act as expert teachers to older people in the community and in doing so break down barriers of misunderstanding,' he said.

International work is so easy to do. I am currently running a project involving 12 schools in eight countries and more than 90 students who are collaborating online in ways which are truly benefiting their schools as well as themselves, and the total cost is nothing except our collective time.

So many good projects flow from a model of education which places the actual practice of skills in equal measure to knowledge.

Currently in the UK creativity is being put head to head in conflict with rigour. This entirely false battle brings up totally biased comparisons, including examples of creative learning which have been poorly constructed pitched against excellent ideals for teaching grammar rules, for example. Such a system will drive the use of ICT further and further from its most useful position. It is entirely possible to provide greater ownership for learners within a framework which is rigorous and challenging.

My fear is that schools will go back to seeing the internet as something for research and not for creative participation, then hundreds of schools will rush out and buy tablets because they are more flashy textbooks and in so doing lock us into this limited model of mobile learning for at least three years.

I want to see a rigorous and challenging approach to developing creativity and problem solving in schools. Just like in real life.

Notes

1 Dewi Lloyd is an education consultant. His Linkedin contact is https://www.linkedin.com/in/dewilloyd and his Twitter handle is @dewilloyd.
2 Dan Buckley is an award-winning educator who established one of the first 1:1 laptop projects in the UK. He has led educational transformation projects in the UK and USA and is currently deputy headteacher at Saltash.net Community College.
3 Saltash.net Community College (http://saltash.net/) is a mixed specialist science, maths and computing 11–18 academy.
4 Personalisation by Pieces (PbyP) is an online assessment tool (developed by Dan Buckley: see note 2 above) for key skills at secondary and primary levels. Using PbyP, teachers can identify learners' skills and capabilities while allowing peer assessment. It has been described as a 'revolutionary tool which opens the door to a new pedagogical paradigm' www.educationimpact.net/home (accessed 14 July 2014).
5 Cambridge Education (www.educationimpact.net/home) is a global pre-university education company and consulting service which manages schools in more than 95 countries.
6 Dave Whyley, learning technologies innovator who led Wolverhampton's Learning2Go project (see below). He is an expert in the effective use of technology in schools.
7 Learning2Go project (www.wolverhampton-engage.net/sites/anonymous/Learning2Go/Pages/default.aspx) is an award-winning approach to mobile learning pioneered by Wolverhampton Education Authority.
8 Becta, former ICT agency responsible for spreading good practice in the use of ICT in UK education. Becta was dissolved by the UK's Coalition Government in what has become known as the 'bonfire of the quangos'.
9 Dr Vanessa Pittard, Policy Lead, Technology Education at the UK's Department for Education and former director of evidence and evaluation at the now defunct national ICT agency Becta (see note 8).
10 Department for Education (DfE), UK government department with responsibility for infant, primary and secondary education: www.education.gov.uk/ (accessed 14 July 2014).
11 BESA (British Education Suppliers Association), the UK's ICT industry trade association: www.besa.org.uk/ (accessed 14 July 2014).
12 Tablets for Schools project, a scheme supported by the UK Government to ensure that all 11-year-olds have access to a digital tablet. It was created by the social responsibility arm of UK mobile phone retailer Carphone Warehouse.
13 Nesta, founded in 1997, is an independent charity that conducts research and provides investment and grants to innovative projects, including inventive ideas in teaching and learning: www.nesta.org.uk/ (accessed 14 July 2014).
14 Education Endowment Foundation, an independent grant-making charity founded by the Sutton Trust, dedicated to breaking the link between family income and educational achievement. It is funded by a £125 million grant from the Department for Education: http://educationendowmentfoundation.org.uk/ (accessed 14 July 2014).
15 Nominet Trust, the UK's only Tech for Good funder. It provides investment to support people who believe in the use of technology to transform the way we address social challenges: www.nominettrust.org.uk/ (accessed 14 July 2014); www.

nominettrust.org.uk/news-events/news/schools-to-test-whether-ipads-texting-and-technology-can-improve-results (accessed 14 July 2014).

16 ACER Institute (Australian Council for Educational Research) runs research-based conferences, workshops and courses for education practitioners and students: www.acerinstitute.edu.au/home (accessed 14 July 2014).

17 Learning Sciences Research Institute (LSRI) is a centre of excellence for research in Learning Sciences and Technology Enhanced Learning at the University of Nottingham. Research at the Institute explores the fundamental processes and practices of learning, and the design of new technologies and environments to enhance learning: www.lsri.nottingham.ac.uk/study/phd (accessed 14 July 2014).

18 Victorian Department of Education and Early Childhood Development: www.education.vic.gov.au/about/contact/Pages/default.aspx (accessed 14 July 2014).

19 DEECD (2012b): *Blended Learning: A Synthesis of Research Findings in Victorian Education*. Melbourne: Department of Education and Early Childhood Development. http://www.eduweb.vic.gov.au/edulibrary/public/researchinnovation/blendedlearning.pdf (accessed 14 July 2014).

20 Hartnell-Young, E & Vetere, F (2008) A means of personalising learning: incorporating old and new literacies in the curriculum with mobile phones. *Curriculum Journal*, 19(4), 283–292.

21 Carol Allen, school improvement adviser for ICT and inclusion in North Tyneside.

22 Green, J, Vetere, F, Nisselle, A, Dang, T, Deng, P & Strong, G (2011) 'Lucy's always with us': overcoming absence from school through ambient orb technology. In: S Barton, J Hedberg & K Suzuki (Eds.) *Proceedings of Global Learn Asia Pacific: Association for the Advancement of Computing in Education (AACE) Global Conference on Learning and Technology*. Melbourne, Australia: Association for the Advancement of Computing in Education (AACE), pp. 1851–1857.

23 Jocelyn Wishart, senior lecturer in education at the Graduate School of Education, University of Bristol.

24 e-Scape project is now being marketed as ACJ and LiveAssess: www.tagassessment.com/acj (accessed 14 July 2014); www.tagassessment.com/liveassess (accessed 14 July 2014); www.gold.ac.uk/teru/projectinfo/projecttitle,5882,en.php (accessed 14 July 2014).

25 Professor Stephen Heppell, award-winning new media expert who, since 1980 has worked with learners, teachers, school leaders and governments to raise the profile of ICT for learning: www.heppell.net (accessed 14 July 2014).

26 Dr Christina Preston, Professor of Educational Innovation at Bedfordshire University and founder of Mirandanet, a community of practice focused on learning and teaching with technology: www.beds.ac.uk/research/ired/groups/dr-christina-preston (accessed 14 July 2014); www.mirandanet.ac.uk/ (accessed 14 July 2014).

27 Mal Lee, education consultant: http://malleehome.com/ (accessed 14 July 2014).

28 Unesco (2005) *Unesco World Report: Toward Knowledge Societies*. Paris: Unesco.

29 Higgins, S, Xiao, ZM & Katsipataki, M (2012) *The Impact of Digital Technology on Learning: A Summary for the Education Endowment Foundation*. http://educationendowmentfoundation.org.uk/uploads/pdf/The_Impact_of_Digital_Technologies_on_Learning_FULL_REPORT_(2012).pdf (accessed 22 July 2014).

CHAPTER

13

Conclusion

The debate is done, the argument over. Handheld devices are sweeping all before them. To transform learning all we need is a highly portable touchscreen with a camera, internet access and a bundle of very clever little programs on a deceptively powerful device. There is nothing more to discuss. Or so it seems.

The drift of technology to mobile devices has been so convincing that it might seem there is nothing left to contest. But the camps rallying behind the various banners, from 1:1, BYOD (bring your own device), BYOT (bring your own technology) through to MOOCs (massive, open online courses), SPOCs (small, private online courses) and VLEs (virtual learning environments), and their underlying interests – supplier, academic, teacher, technophile, developer – mean that the debate continues to be rich and at times heated. Its clamour can be hard to ignore. Like a TV channel surfer during the Olympics, there is simply no getting away from it. It demands your attention.

Perhaps this is the residue of the generous ICT budgets of the last Labour government, spending £2.5 billion in its first ten years, from 1997 to 2007, with continued spending peaking at £586 million in 2009.[1] But then the Coalition Government came along, distinguished by its lack of interest in teaching and technology. The Damascene moment came in 2014 with the creation of its Educational Technology Action Group (ETAG) – and now it seems to 'get it'. But what is there to get? What do learners, teachers and schools want?

Some want the technology but don't, apparently, know why. They don't fully appreciate what it offers, and the opportunities it can bring. Others 'get' the opportunity to carry on as before but more efficiently and presented in shiny new packaging with better bells and shriller whistles. The ones who really 'get' it have been waiting for this chance and see technology as the driver for more fundamental changes in teaching and learning – in traditional classroom relationships and in the balance of responsibilities in schools.

And why this technology? Why mobiles and handhelds? Why should we believe it is different this time? Will our hopes for transformation in classrooms be dashed again, as with other technologies? Is it new technology we need, or new approaches to education? Or does one inevitably bring about the other, only varying in degree across establishments in the impact we see?

Schools have been subjected to a number of 'orthodoxies', for example, a whiteboard in every class, and many of these have been brought in by government–industry partnerships to help bring schools to the 'tipping point' where technology for learning is ubiquitous and used appropriately and naturally. But those days are over, and schools have never been in a better position to make their own choices based on their own needs. There is no right way, just the one that suits their needs. Sadly there are perhaps not 'wrong' but certainly misguided ways – ones that could lead them up a technology blind alley, wasting valuable resources.

One thing that seems clear is that mobiles and handhelds are being more widely used by both teachers and learners alike than any other technology to date. It could be their availability, or their speed to activity once the start button is pushed, although it is also quite probable that it is their simplicity. Unlike interactive whiteboards there is no need for extensive, expensive, training courses to bring people up to speed on how to use this kit. We all have anecdotes of previously technologically averse people – frequently the elderly – who are now connecting online with others, mainly family, because of the simplicity of the devices and the fact that they can use them anywhere in the home. Handheld technologies have a shallow learning curve with multiple applications, coupled with a minimal investment of time and effort to get a high return of opportunity and potential.

You don't have to be an 'early adopter' to benefit from these innovations, nor even be near the front of the field. Some people will kick off instantly to new and exciting things while others use technology to do the old things differently, explore the possibilities and then move on from there. You don't have to do something amazing the moment you pick up a digital device. You can be the tortoise and let the hares race ahead in the understanding that you may well overtake. And this digital revolution isn't just for geeks – the ones who love the tech for its own sake. It's for non-geeks too – the ones who are more interested in what these devices can do, things that are different and interesting – and it is they who will probably benefit the most.

Practitioners with a passion for learning and teaching might want to gather lots of ideas for what to do with digital tools. They shouldn't be put off dipping their toes in for a moderate start that may lead to something great. A teacher who loves technology and jumps at using it at every opportunity might miss the obvious benefits that incremental steps can give, and lack the fluency with pedagogy that could bring real innovation.

Embracing a particular technology doesn't seem to matter too much, either. There are a number of options, even if one – the iPad, designed for individual use and conscripted into institutional duty – leads the parade. But this doesn't mean the choice of device, or more importantly, operating system, is immaterial. Each has its functions, services and affordances. Each also has its means to tie users in and keep them engaged, through familiarity, preference, loyalty or, perhaps cynically, dependency.

Even if we can perceive this movement as device, platform or brand agnostic, we can still question what role technology has at all in suggestions of seismic shifts in teaching and learning. Change can only happen if teachers let it happen. In learning establishments where they won't, learners remain passive. In schools where they do, learners will be integral to the process. Although the argument remains that this is not a shift that can be entirely controlled. Just as the invention of the printing press and mass production of books made information available to large numbers of people, knowledge that previously had been filtered, and censored, by an elite in the church and the universities, so the latest technologies are continuing to build on the revolution in access to information, and the tools to inform.

The statistics are mind-boggling.[2] People who could formerly count their real friends on two hands might now have hundreds of friends on Facebook (the average is 200!), or thousands of followers on Twitter. For those with little to say, that could be just a greater opportunity to contribute to a general digital clamour. But for educators, and learners, needing networks for communicating and sharing?

By the end of 2013 Facebook had 1.23 billion global users monthly (757 million of them logging on daily). In the UK 24 million people (more than a third of the population) log on every day, although the number of users has fallen slightly over a year – by around 1.5 million to 31,456,000 – roughly half the UK population.

Social media services are inextricably linked to the media sites for video and photo uploading which drive a lot of the activity. Facebook bought one of them, Instagram, with 135 million users, for £1 billion and now it also owns the popular Whatsapp media messaging service.

Google doesn't release data about its Google+ social media service, which is thought to be the second most popular after Facebook, but its YouTube site is another stunner for statistics. Take these from spring 2014:

- More than 1 billion unique users visit YouTube each month, watching more than 6 billion hours of video.

- 100 hours of video are uploaded to YouTube every minute.

- YouTube is available on hundreds of devices and mobile makes up 'almost 40 per cent of YouTube's global watch time'.[3]

Some estimates for the percentage of mobile users of social media are as high as 60 per cent, and it is thought that 80 per cent of Twitter subscribers use mobile.

From these figures, it's clear that the activities that were once the preserve of people using desktop computers are now moving over to mobile. Developing countries with limited infrastructure are skipping a stage and accessing the internet by mobile devices. Kenya, for example, has already pioneered the use of mobile phones for micro-payments. Now UK banks are bringing in payment schemes for mobile phone users.

United Nations Educational, Scientific and Cultural Organisation (Unesco) reckons that 774 million adults and 123 million young people in the world can't read or write, and that one of their problems is no access to text. So it's no surprise that it conducted a survey, *Reading in the Mobile Era: A Study of Mobile Reading in Developing Countries* (with Nokia and Worldreader).[4]

In developing countries mobile broadband coverage reaches around 20 per cent of people (11 per cent in Africa). The Unesco survey – 'the most comprehensive investigation of mobile reading in developing countries to date' – was completed by more than 4,000 people in seven countries (Ethiopia, Ghana, India, Kenya, Nigeria, Pakistan and Zimbabwe).

It found that 'people seem to enjoy reading more when they use mobile devices to access text'. For those who already liked reading, 'mobile reading reinforced and amplified those dispositions'. 'For people who disliked or hated reading prior to reading on their mobile phones, the experience tended to change their attitude towards reading for the better.'

The report's key conclusion was that:

> Mobile devices constitute one tool – in a repertoire of other tools – that can help people develop, sustain and enhance their literacy skills. They can help people find good books and, gradually, cultivate a love of reading along with the myriad advantages that portends – educationally, socially and economically.

Looking to the future, the report added, 'A revolution in reading is upon us thanks to the massive proliferation of mobile technology, and future research should aim to evaluate, improve and facilitate this revolution as it unfolds.' Readers should bear in mind that this survey was not about high-end smartphones, but phones accessible in those developing countries.

The growth in communication media and content production has been phenomenal and the role of mobile devices is now mainstream. And it's no longer just one device. A smartphone will do most things but tablets bring improvements and laptops even more for those who need keyboard control and bigger screens.

This has happened whether or not it can be exploited in schools, which is why mobile technology is second nature to most young people and many older people too.

We can suggest that increased availability of technology gives greater openness and access, and thereby accountability, to us all, with more opportunities to connect, communicate and create. And the ubiquity of handheld and mobile technologies further extends and amplifies this.

We can also argue that some changes can't happen without the technology providing ways of creating, curating, cooperating, collaborating, challenging and choosing – powerful tools in our pockets, like digital Swiss Army knives. Everyone can be a film-maker, composer, author, blogger, friend and opinion leader, so text need no longer prevail as the overweening medium for demonstrating learning.

However, these tools are often rudimentary and incapable of creating a properly polished final product, rather as a penknife is to a mitre saw, designed for rough-and-ready whittling rather than precision and finesse. If we want to write a novel, remake *Gone with the Wind*, compose a concerto or even program an app, we may need something else. One device is unlikely to do it all. One to one might not be enough. Tablets are not taking over completely from desktops and laptops – they may be supplanting some or supplementing others, but they are an additiona. technological option, not a direct replacement.

One area where these additional opportunities have been willingly taken up is special educational needs, a field where problem solving is embedded in practice, finding answers to the ongoing questions about communication and curriculum access raised by every individual's divers, personal learning needs.

Here mobile devices have brought what were once highly specialised technologies – touch sensitivity, speech feedback, voice control, proximity sensors – into the mainstream, which has resulted in falls in the sales of more specialist products. Why buy something that has a specific, but limited, use, when a highly desirable, lifestyle-enhancing, flexible gadget will suffice just as well? Not that these users show tribal loyalty to one brand; their needs are the focus and whatever best removes barriers will be their choice.

For these teachers, and their learners, the adoption of the latest technology is something they take in their stride. A new opportunity is offered, which is taken up and appropriated to their specific ends, often with life-enhancing outcomes. With the overly enthusiastic, tablets are seen as a panacea, an electronic elixir that will ease any impediment to learning. Yet too often they can become a digital sedative, a means to engage in activities where that engagement can be easily, but not always accurately, interpreted as 'learning'.

Which raises one of the most fundamental questions about the use of handhelds and mobiles in schools. How do we know that learners really are learning, and that what we are witnessing is an improvement in educational outcomes? How can we be sure the devices are not a distracting sideshow, as suspected by some parents, a section of the public, and possibly some policy makers too?

Objective analysis can provide figures to show changes in attainment due to the adoption of handheld and mobile technologies, but the most influential source of evidence we have is the testimony of teachers that classrooms are changing for the better because tablets and mobiles have made their entrance. So is it time to accept them and the positive benefits they bring, rather than ban them as sources of disruption and distraction?

Looking through the case studies in this book you will find examples of the features (maybe even all of them in the activities of Apps for Good) – learning partners using technology 'to construct knowledge, to investigate and solve real problems, to give each other feedback and assess one another's work, to collaborate beyond the boundaries of the classroom and the school day, and to communicate with peers, experts and others throughout the world'.[5] It is no coincidence that these features, enabled by the use of technology, are part of the analysis of the 'new pedagogies' outlined in *A Rich Seam: How New Pedagogies Find Deep Learning*, the 2014 paper commissioned by Pearson from education reformer Michael Fullan and researcher Maria Langworthy.

Michael Fullan, professor emeritus at the Ontario Institute for Studies in Education at the University of Toronto, believes that a revolution in education is already happening and will have affected everyone within five years, whether they want to acknowledge it or not. His advice is to approach the disruption and

, working through the change. And he is working with 1,000 schools
: to model the new pedagogies and deep learning and to share them.
website he says:[6]

e been working on educational change for almost 50 years. There is
thing different about 2014. There is a grand convergence spontaneously
erupting. I think it is a natural dynamic of push and pull. The push, to put
it directly, is a combination of the boredom and alienation of students and
teachers. Students won't wait, and teachers can't wait. It is simply intolerable
for students and teachers to be at school every day when increasing numbers
of them would rather be somewhere else. What kind of existence is that!

On the other hand the digital world is a 24/7 phenomenon of limitless
intrigue and consternation. There is something out there but it cannot be
fathomed. Humans have stopped evolving physically, but the brain is changing
in uncontainable ways. Humankind's relationship to the universe is becoming
seamless. There is no distinction between us and mother nature; between us
and what we are creating – digitally, artistically, and spontaneously. We are
what we create, and what incubates ineluctably becomes us.

We are seeing combustions that are as inevitable as they are mysterious. They
are unstoppable. This is what I have called The Stratosphere.[7] Technology,
pedagogy and change dynamics are converging on their own. We cannot stop
them but we can take advantage of them to enable and accelerate learning,
where learning and living become indistinguishable. This is not a theoretical
realm. It is reality.

The new furrows being tilled by the likes of Michael Fullan are truly exciting. His
sometime collaborator, academic Andy Hargreaves, described Stratosphere as 'the
best thing I have read on technology and education'. With the talk about 'new
pedagogies' it's also clear that technology, and mobile in particular, give new life
and vigour to aspects of pedagogy that have long been recognised as powerful, and
for which there is plentiful evidence of effectiveness – just take peer learning and
assessment, for example.

It's time for change, to revisit some fundamental tenets of the education system
and move to a different paradigm. Whether following or leading, technology is
integral to the shift.

It is a situation many educators have been seeking for a considerable time, and
one in which technology will also be key to spreading the message. Legendary
education reformer John Dewey (1859–1952)[8] recognised this need:

A society which is mobile, which is full of channels for the distribution of a
change occurring anywhere, must see to it that its members are educated to
personal initiative and adaptability. Otherwise, they will be overwhelmed by
the changes in which they are caught and whose significance or connections
they do not perceive.

Notes

1 BESA: www.besa.org.uk (accessed 28 July 2014).

2 Rose, K (2014) *UK Social Media Statistics for 2014.* http://socialmediatoday.com/kate-rose-mcgrory/2040906/uk-social-media-statistics-2014 (accessed 28 July 2014).

3 YouTube statistics: https://www.youtube.com/yt/press/en-GB/statistics.html (accessed 29 July 2014).

4 Unesco (2014) *Reading in the Mobile Area: A Study of Mobile Reading in Developing Countries.* http://unesdoc.unesco.org/images/0022/002274/227436e.pdf (accessed 28 July 2014).

5 Fullan, M & Langworthy, M (2014) *A Rich Seam: How New Pedagogies Find Deep Learning.* http://www.michaelfullan.ca/wp-content/uploads/2014/01/3897.Rich_Seam_web.pdf (accessed 29 July 2014).

6 Michael Fullan: www.michaelfullan.ca/there-is-something-different-about-2014/ (accessed 28 July 2014).

7 Fullan, M (2012) *Stratosphere: Integrating Technology, Pedagogy, and Change Knowledge.* www.pearsoncanadaschool.com/index.cfm?locator=PS1zR4&PMDbSiteId=2621&PMDbSolutionId=25862&PMDbSubSolutionId=&PMDbCategoryId=25878&PMDbSubCategoryId=26071&PMDbSubjectAreaId=&PMDbProgramId=100981 (accessed 28 July 2014).

8 John Dewey, 1916: http://en.wikiquote.org/wiki/John_Dewey (accessed 28 July 2014).

Bibliography

ACER Institute (Australian Council for Educational Research) runs research-based conferences, workshops and courses for education practitioners and students: www. acerinstitute.edu.au/home (accessed 14 July 2014).

Agent4change.net. Looking for Inspiration? Make your School the Source. http:// agent4change.net/innovation/innovation/2073 (accessed 14 July 2014).

Agent4change.net. World's First EDA for Schools. http://agent4change.net/resources/ hardware/57 (accessed 14 July 2014).

Apple Distinguished Educators (www.apple.com/uk/education/apple-distinguished-educator/) is a global community of more than 2,000 education leaders recognised by Apple as doing innovative work with the company's technology, in and out of the classroom.

Apps for Good: http://www.appsforgood.org/ (accessed 28 July 2014).

Apps for Good 2013 award winners: www.appsforgood.org/public/student-apps (accessed 28 July 2014).

Aurasma (www.aurasma.com/). The Aurasma 'augmented-reality' app was launched in 2011 with a vision 'to enable an augmented world, where every image, object and place has its own Aura'. It has more than 40,000 customers in over 100 countries.

BCS – The Chartered Institute for IT: www.bcs.org/ (accessed 14 July 2014).

Becta (Wikipedia): http://en.wikipedia.org/wiki/Becta (accessed 14 July 2014).

BESA (British Education Suppliers Association) is the UK's ICT industry trade association: www.besa.org.uk/ (accessed 14 July 2014).

BESA (British Educational Suppliers Association). *Procurement in Authority, Schools and Academies, Part 1: View from Schools.* www.besa.org.uk/library?title=&field_ document_type_tid=211 (accessed 14 July 2014); www.besa.org.uk/ (accessed 14 July 2014).

BESA (2013) *Increasing Expectation on Publishers to Develop Tablet Apps.* http://www.besa. org.uk/news/besa-press-release-increasing-expectation-publishers-develop-tablet-apps (accessed 28 July 2014).

BESA (2013) *Tablets and Apps in School 2013.* http://www.besa.org.uk/sites/default/files/ tab2013_0.pdf (accessed 28 July 2014).

BESA (2014) *Resources in English Maintained Schools.* http://www.besa.org.uk/sites/ default/files/ess2014_volii_0.pdf (accessed 28 July 2014)

Building Schools for the Future (BSF) was an ambitious £55 billion secondary school rebuilding and renovation programme in England, put in place by the Blair Government. It was overseen by Partnership for Schools, a non-departmental joint venture between the Department for Children, Schools and Families (now the Department for Education), Partnerships UK and private-sector partners. BSF was controversially axed in 2010 by the incoming Education Secretary, Michael Gove, with the explanation that 'it was wasteful and bureaucratic'.

Burden, K, Hopkins, P, Male, M, Martin, S & Trala, C (Faculty of Education, The University of Hull). *iPad Scotland Evaluation*. www2.hull.ac.uk/ifl/ipadresearchinschools.aspx (accessed 14 July 2014).

Cambridge Education (www.educationimpact.net/home) is a global pre-university education company and consulting service which manages schools in more than 95 countries.

Carl Faulkner's awards for his pioneering work with mobile technology: *Gazette Live*, 10 May 2010: www.gazettelive.co.uk/news/local-news/normanby-primary-school-headteacher-honoured-3704522 (accessed 14 July 2014).

Carl Faulkner's Handheld Learning Primary Practitioner and Primary Innovation award: Agent4change.net, 6 October 2009: www.agent4change.net/events/awards/419-teachers-in-the-frame-at-handheld-learning-09-awards.html (accessed 14 July 2014).

Cattle Manager app: https://play.google.com/store/apps/details?id=com.catman (accessed 28 July 2014).

CIA World Factbook is an expansive body of international data that is collected from a variety of US Government agencies and hundreds of published sources. It is presented on The World Factbook website which is updated every week (www.cia.gov) (accessed 30 April 2014).

Computing curriculum for English schools: www.gov.uk/government/publications/national-curriculum-in-england-computing-programmes-of-study (accessed 14 July 2014).

Cramlington Learning Village: www.cramlingtonlv.co.uk/ (accessed 14 July 2014).

Cramlington Learning Village (2012) *It's not Just Geordie Shore*. www.amazon.co.uk/Its-just-Geordie-Shore-ebook/dp/B008FDWP52 (accessed 14 July 2014).

Creative Education's 'Top Twitter Hashtags for Teachers'

Cuban, L. A Second Look at iPads in Los Angeles. http://larrycuban.wordpress.com/2013/12/06/a-second-look-at-ipads-in-los-angeles/ (accessed 14 July 2014).

Culture Lab at Newcastle University: http://www.ncl.ac.uk/culturelab/ (accessed 14 July 2014).

Daily Mail. Every School Child in Los Angeles to Get an iPad. www.dailymail.co.uk/news/article-2345124/EVERY-school-child-Los-Angeles-iPad-state-strikes-30m-deal-Apple.html (accessed 14 July 2014).

Dawn Hallybone presents her work at Learning Without Frontiers: www.youtube.com/watch?v=Qx9nbSK8V5w (accessed 14 July 2014).

Dawn Hallybone's pioneering work with handheld devices: http://agent4change.net/innovators/580-the-innovators-15-dawn-hallybone.html (accessed 14 July 2014); http://agent4change.net/events/awards/419-teachers-in-the-frame-at-handheld-learning-09-awards.html (accessed 14 July 2014).

DEECD (2012): *Blended Learning: A Synthesis of Research Findings in Victorian Education.* Melbourne: Department of Education and Early Childhood Development. http://www.eduweb.vic.gov.au/edulibrary/public/researchinnovation/blendedlearning.pdf (accessed 14 July 2014).

Dog Log: https://play.google.com/store/apps/details?id=com.afga.doglog (accessed 28 July 2014).

Dr Christina Preston, Professor of Educational Innovation at Bedfordshire University and founder of Mirandanet, a community of practice focused on learning and teaching with technology:
www.beds.ac.uk/research/ired/groups/dr-christina-preston (accessed 14 July 2014); www.mirandanet.ac.uk/ (accessed 14 July 2014).

Department for Education (DfE), UK government department with responsibility for infant, primary and secondary education: www.education.gov.uk/ (accessed 14 July 2014).

Developer Economics Q3 2013, State of the Developer Nation, the fifth in a series of research documents tracking the mobile developer economy, sponsored by Blackberry and Mozilla, published July 2013, www.developereconomics.com/reports/q3–2013/ (accessed 14 July 2014).

Dewi Lloyd is an education consultant. His Linkedin contact is https://www.linkedin.com/in/dewilloyd and his Twitter handle is @dewilloyd.

Down syndrome, also known as Down's syndrome, is a genetic condition that causes some level of learning disability and a characteristic range of physical features, www.downs-syndrome.org.uk/ (accessed 14 July 2014).

Early Childhood Development. http://www.eduweb.vic.gov.au/edulibrary/public/researchinnovation/blendedlearning.pdf (accessed 14 July 2014).

easyvote: www.easyvote.co.uk/ (accessed 14 July 2014).

eClicker is an iPad app that allows teachers to conduct formative assessments with students in their classroom, collect individual responses and summarise class results. These can then be shared and students can receive feedback on their own responses, later reviewed by the teacher: http://eclicker.com/ (accessed 14 July 2014).

EdFutures (http://edfutures.net/) is a website dedicated to supporting change of the current education system, with a focus on the role that technology might play as a leader for change (or Trojan mouse). It is run by Professor Peter Twining, a senior lecturer at the Open University.

Education Endowment Foundation (http://educationendowmentfoundation.org.uk) is an independent grant-making charity founded by the Sutton Trust, dedicated to breaking the link between family income and educational achievement. It is funded by a £125 million grant from the Department for Education and is run by the Sutton Trust with support from the Impetus Trust.

Eduinnova: www.theguardian.com/education/2007/jun/19/elearning.technology9 (accessed 30 April 2014).

e-Learning Foundation (http://www.e-learningfoundation.com/), which launched in 2001, works in partnership with schools, parents, charities and businesses to provide computers, educational software and internet access to all schoolchildren, especially those from disadvantaged backgrounds and with special learning needs.

e-Learning Foundation tablets literature review: Thompson, V (2013) *Literature Review: Evidence of Impact of 1:1 Access to Tablet Computers in the Classroom.* http://creative.eun.org/c/document_library/get_file?uuid=f90beb15-d561–4ed3–9f50–929c4b899a1b&groupId=96459 (accessed 28 July 2014).

e-Scape project is now being marketed as ACJ and LiveAssess: www.tagassessment.com/acj (accessed 14 July 2014); www.tagassessment.com/liveassess (accessed 14 July 2014); www.gold.ac.uk/teru/projectinfo/projecttitle,5882,en.php (accessed 14 July 2014).

Essa Foundation (www.essaacademy.org/) is an education charity set up to encourage research, development and introduction of best practice across schools and the curriculum, for use by headteachers, staff, governing bodies and students in schools in the UK and worldwide.

Flitch Green, Dunmow, Essex, UK: http://theflitchgreenacademy.co.uk/ (accessed 14 July 2014).

Frank Wise School, Banbury, Oxfordshire: http://www.frankwise.oxon.sch.uk/ (accessed 14 July 2014).

Fullan, M (2012) *Stratosphere: Integrating Technology, Pedagogy, and Change Knowledge.* www.pearsoncanadaschool.com/index.cfm?locator=PS1zR4&PMDbSiteId=2621&PMDbSolutionId=25862&PMDbSubSolutionId=&PMDbCategoryId=25878&PMDbSubCategoryId=26071&PMDbSubjectAreaId=&PMDbProgramId=100981 (accessed 28 July 2014).

Fullan, M & Langworthy, M (2013) *New Pedagogies for Deep Learning.* www.michaelfullan.ca/wp-content/uploads/2013/08/New-Pedagogies-for-Deep-Learning-An-Invitation-to-Partner-2013–6–201.pdf (accessed 14 July 2014).

Fullan, M & Langworthy, M (2014) *A Rich Seam: How New Pedagogies Find Deep Learning.* http://www.michaelfullan.ca/wp-content/uploads/2014/01/3897.Rich_Seam_web.pdf (accessed 29 July 2014).

Gartner predictions for 2014 (Reuters): www.reuters.com/article/2014/01/07/us-mobile-devices-gartner-idUSBREA060E220140107 (accessed 14 July 2014); www.gartner.com/technology/home.jsp (accessed 14 July 2014).

Genius Bar is the technology support station found in every retail store owned by American technology giant Apple. Employees are trained and certified at the Genius Bar to offer help to customers with their Apple hardware and software: www.apple.com/uk/retail/geniusbar/ (accessed 14 July 2014).

Gove speech to BETT 2012: www.gov.uk/government/speeches/michael-gove-speech-at-the-bett-show-2012 (accessed 14 July 2014).

Green, J, Vetere, F, Nisselle, A, Dang, T, Deng, P & Strong, G (2011) 'Lucy's always with us': overcoming absence from school through ambient orb technology. In: S Barton, J Hedberg & K Suzuki (Eds.) *Proceedings of Global Learn Asia Pacific: Association for the Advancement of Computing in Education (AACE) Global Conference on Learning and Technology.* Melbourne, Australia: Association for the Advancement of Computing in Education (AACE), pp. 1851–1857.

GSMA *Mobile Economy Report* (2013) www.gsma.com/ (accessed 22 July 2014).

GSMA *Mobile Education Landscape Report* (2011) This report describes emerging trends, key players and current initiatives in the emerging mobile education and related e-textbook publishing market. www.gsma.com/ (accessed 22 July 2014).

GSMA *Mobile Proposition for Education* (2012) This report describes educational scenarios where the use of mobile-enabled handheld technologies can deliver significant benefits and the assets and the expertise the mobile ecosystem can offer the education sector. www.gsma.com/ (accessed 22 July 2014).

GSMA *Safeguarding Security and Privacy in Mobile Education* (2012) www.gsma.com/ (accessed 22 July 2014).

Hartnell-Young, E & Vetere, F (2008) A means of personalising learning: incorporating old and new literacies in the curriculum with mobile phones. *Curriculum Journal*, 19(4), 283–292.

Heppell.net is run by Professor Stephen Heppell, award-winning new media expert who, since 1980, has worked with learners, teachers, school leaders and governments to raise the profile of ICT for learning: www.heppell.net (accessed 14 July 2014).

Higgins, S, Xiao, ZM & Katsipataki, M (2012) *The Impact of Digital Technology on Learning: A Summary for the Education Endowment Foundation.* http://educationen dowmentfoundation.org.uk/uploads/pdf/The_Impact_of_Digital_Technologies_ on_Learning_FULL_REPORT_(2012).pdf (accessed 22 July 2014).

How to 'self-publish': https://www.lulu.com/ (accessed 14 July 2014).

iPads in the Classroom 2013, published by the London Knowledge Lab, Institute of Education, written by Wilma Clark and Rosemary Luckin, www.lkl.ac.uk/cms/ index.php?option=com_events&task=view_detail&Itemid=108&agid=315

Iris Connect classroom system for recording, analysing and sharing classroom practice: http://www.irisconnect.co.uk/ (accessed 14 July 2014).

iWise media centre was opened in 2009 (www.frankwise.oxon.sch.uk). It is a state-of-the-art suite of rooms with one large teaching space and meeting room, its own cafe area, fully equipped sound studio, green-screen space and an animation studio.

John Dewey, 1916: http://en.wikiquote.org/wiki/John_Dewey (accessed 28 July 2014).

Learning Sciences Research Institute (LSRI) is a centre of excellence for research in Learning Sciences and Technology Enhanced Learning at the University of Nottingham. Research at the Institute explores the fundamental processes and practices of learning, and the design of new technologies and environments to enhance learning: www.lsri.nottingham.ac.uk/study/phd (accessed 14 July 2014).

Learning Without Frontiers (www.learningwithoutfrontiers.com/) was conceived in 2004 as an annual gathering of education innovation which included a conference and awards ceremony. It closed in 2013.

Learning2Go project (www.wolverhampton-engage.net/sites/anonymous/Learning2Go/ Pages/default.aspx) is an award-winning approach to mobile learning pioneered by Wolverhampton Education Authority.

Leask, M & Meadows, J (eds) (2000) *Teaching and Learning with ICT in the Primary School.* London: Routledge Falmer.

Littler, M (2014) Touch and Pads Open Door to SEN 'Dream Device'. Agent4change.net: http://agent4change.net/inclusion/inclusion/2106 (accessed 14 July 2014).

Mal Lee, education consultant: http://malleehome.com/ (accessed 14 July 2014).

Maths Ninja: https://itunes.apple.com/gb/app/math-ninja-hd-free!/id373814902?mt=8 (accessed 14 July 2014).

McFarlane, A, Roche, N & Triggs, P (2007) *Mobile Learning: Research Findings.* Report to Becta. http://dera.ioe.ac.uk/1470/1/becta_2007_mobilelearning_interim_report. pdf (accessed 14 July 2014).

Metro. Kent School Gives an iPad to Each of its 1,400 Pupils. http://metro.co.uk/2011/07/ 14/kent-school-gives-an-ipad-to-each-of-its-1400-pupils-77258/ (accessed 14 July 2014).

Michael Fullan: www.michaelfullan.ca/there-is-something-different-about-2014/ (accessed 28 July 2014).

Mirandanet, a community of practice focused on learning and teaching with technology founded by Dr Christina Preston, Professor of Educational Innovation at Bedfordshire University: www.beds.ac.uk/research/ired/groups/dr-christina-preston (accessed 14 July 2014); www.mirandanet.ac.uk/ (accessed 14 July 2014).

MJO Online/Agent4Change.net (www.agent4change.net) is a UK-based online source of information on technology for learning aimed at education professionals. It provides high-quality original news, features, analysis and reviews from a range of contributors and commentators, and is an independent title not affiliated to a trade or professional body.

Naace (http://www.naace.co.uk/) is a national ICT association made up of educators, technologists and policy makers who wish to advance both teaching and learning through the use of technology.

Naace ICT Impact Awards (2012) Supporting Inclusion in Any Phase. http://www.naace. co.uk/events/conference2012/naaceimpactawards2012/winners (accessed 14 July 2014).

Nesta, founded in 1997, is an independent charity that conducts research and provides investment and grants to innovative projects, including inventive ideas in teaching and learning: www.nesta.org.uk/ (accessed 14 July 2014).

Nominet Trust, the UK's only Tech for Good funder. It provides investment to support people who believe in the use of technology to transform the way we address social challenges: www.nominettrust.org.uk/ (accessed 14 July 2014); www.nominettrust. org.uk/news-events/news/schools-to-test-whether-ipads-texting-and-technology-can-improve-results (accessed 14 July 2014).

Normanby Primary School: www.redcar-cleveland.gov.uk/normanbyprimary (accessed 14 July 2014).

Northern Grid For Learning Awards 2011. http://www.northerngrid.org/resource/woodlawn-case-study (accessed 14 July 2014).

Novoda: http://novoda.com/ (accessed 28 July 2014).

Oakdale Junior School: www.oakdalejuniors.co.uk (accessed 14 July 2014).

Organisation for Economic Co-operation and Development (OECD) works with governments to understand what drives economic, social and environmental change. It measures productivity and global flows of trade and investment and analyses and compares data to predict future trends. It is also responsible for setting international standards on a wide range of things, from agriculture and tax to the safety of chemicals.

Online courses written by Normanby staff and hosted through iTunes U: https://itunes. apple.com/gb/course/normanby-primary-school-foundation/id584760731 (accessed 14 July 2014); https://itunes.apple.com/gb/course/normanby-primary-ibooks/id665806534 (accessed 14 July 2014); https://itunes.apple.com/gb/course/world-war-ii-for-upper-key/id584760128 (accessed 14 July 2014); https://itunes. apple.com/gb/course/pirates/id586897578 (accessed 14 July 2014); https://itunes. apple.com/gb/course/year-6-handbook-guide-for/id584760476 (accessed 14 July 2014); https://itunes.apple.com/gb/course/transport/id586898826 (accessed 14 July 2014); https://itunes.apple.com/gb/course/parent-and-carer-guide-to-y5/id586895739 (accessed 14 July 2014); https://itunes.apple.com/gb/course/ancient-greeks/id586893580 (accessed 14 July 2014).

Personalisation by Pieces (PbyP) is an online assessment tool (developed by Dan Buckley) for key skills at secondary and primary levels. Using PbyP, teachers can identify learners' skills and capabilities while allowing peer assessment. It has been described

as a 'revolutionary tool which opens the door to a new pedagogical paradigm' www.
educationimpact.net/home (accessed 14 July 2014).

Plant Pot: http://plantpot.co/ (accessed 28 July 2014).

Pokemon: Typing Adventure and Art Academy: www.nintendo.com/games (accessed 14
July 2014).

PopMath: https://itunes.apple.com/gb/app/id295536766?mt=8 (accessed 14 July 2014).

Professor Layton: http://professorlayton.nintendo.com/ (accessed 14 July 2014).

Quick response (QR) code is text that has been encoded in a two-dimensional barcode
format that can be read by smartphones and tablets (http://en.wikipedia.org/wiki/
QR_code).

Redbridge Games Network: http://redbridgegamesnetwork.blogspot.co.uk/ (accessed 14
July 2014).

RMS Titanic was, in its time, the largest passenger ship in the world. It sank in the North
Atlantic on its maiden voyage in 1912, killing 1,490 people (www.rmstitanic.net/).

Rose, K (2014) *UK Social Media Statistics for 2014.* http://socialmediatoday.com/kate-rose-
mcgrory/2040906/uk-social-media-statistics-2014 (accessed 28 July 2014).

Royal Academy of Engineering: www.raeng.org.uk/ (accessed 14 July 2014).

Saltash.net Community College (http://saltash.net/) is a mixed specialist science, maths
and computing 11–18 academy.

Scott, D & Usher, R (1999) *Researching Education.* London: Institute of Education. See
www.ioe.ac.uk/staff/cpat/lccn_74.html (accessed 14 July 2014); www.bloomsbury.
com/author/robin-usher (accessed 14 July 2014).

StoryPhones (www.storyphones.co.uk/) is an MP3 digital audio system with headsets and
a remote control that primary schoolchildren can use to listen to stories, sing along
to songs, join in listening games, learn new languages and even record their own
stories to share.

Tablets for Schools (www.tabletsforschools.org.uk/) is a scheme supported by the UK
Government to ensure that all 11-year-olds have access to a digital tablet. It is a
campaigning organisation that regularly conducts independent research around the
use of tablet computers in school. Launched in 2012, it is supported by headteachers,
schools, leading academics, charities, industry and Government. Supporters and
partners include a number of household names in the technology field, including
Google, Sony, Samsung, Microsoft and ICT associations Naace and the e-Learning
Foundation. It was created by the social responsibility arm of UK mobile phone
retailer Carphone Warehouse.

Tablets for Schools (2012) *One-to-One Tablets in Secondary Schools: An Evaluation Study. Stage
1: 2011–2012.* http://tabletsforschools.adheredev.com/wp-content/uploads/2012/
12/2011–12-Final-Report.pdf (accessed 28 July 2014).

Tablets for Schools (2013) *One-to-One Tablets in Secondary Schools: An Evaluation Study. Stage
2: January–April 2013.* http://tabletsforschools.org.uk/wp-content/uploads/2012/12/
FKY-Tablets-for-Schools-Stage-2-Full-Report-July-2013.pdf (accessed 28 July 2014).

TechCrunch (2013) Google's Chromebooks Have Hit Their Stride. http://techcrunch.
com/2013/12/28/googles-chromebooks-have-hit-their-stride/ (accessed 14 July 2014).

Techradar (www.techradar.com), one of five websites owned by Future, an award-winning
media group. This website carries reviews and news features on the latest technology
products, including home entertaining and mobile phones (cell phones).

TES is a weekly magazine aimed at teachers and further education lecturers and was first
published in the UK in 1910. The publication has changed ownership several times

since 2005, and is currently owned by TPG Capital LLP, a global private investment firm. *TES* has a readership of more than 350,000 and includes a website (www.tes. co.uk) with more than 2.7 million registered users.

TES schools annual awards (www.tesawards.co.uk/) recognise and reward the work of individual and teams of teachers.

Tesco Hudl tablet: http://www.tesco.com/direct/hudl/ (accessed 14 July 2014).

The Communication Market 2013 (August): http://stakeholders.ofcom.org.uk/market-data-research/market-data/communications-market-reports/cmr13/?a=0 (accessed 14 July 2014).

The New Basics curriculum is said to be 'transdisciplinary' and 'futures-oriented' as it allows students to cover all areas of knowledge at GCSE level and beyond, while tackling real-life issues such as organising community events (www.eqa.edu.au/site/forwardtonewbasics.html; accessed 14 July 2014).

The Office for Standards in Education, Children's Services and Skills (Ofsted) (http://www.ofsted.gov.uk/) is a non-ministerial watchdog responsible for regulating and carrying out regular inspections of state schools, colleges, child minding and daycare in England. Since 2007 Ofsted has also provided inspection for social care services for children and the welfare inspection of independent and maintained boarding schools.

Tony Lennox: www.treasuretrails.co.uk/ (accessed 14 July 2014).

Top Twitter Hashtags for Teachers: www.creativeeducation.co.uk/blog/index.php/2010/12/top-twitter-hashtags-for-uk-teachers/ (accessed 22 July 2014).

Unesco (2005) *Unesco World Report: Toward Knowledge Societies*. Paris: Unesco.

Unesco (2014) *Reading in the Mobile Area*. http://unesdoc.unesco.org/images/0022/002274/227436e.pdf (accessed 28 July 2014).

Unesco case study: http://www.Unesco.org/education/lwf/doc/portfolio/case2.htm (accessed 14 July 2014).

Victorian Department of Education and Early Childhood Development: www.education.vic.gov.au/about/contact/Pages/default.aspx (accessed 14 July 2014).

Which? (also known as the Consumers' Association) was set up in 1957 and is well known for its product testing and consumer campaigning. The UK-based independent charity, which includes a magazine and website (www.which.co.uk), is funded solely by subscriptions to support its advocacy campaigns and consumer protection work. It prides itself on not accepting 'advertising, freebies or government funding'. See www.which.co.uk/tabletsize (accessed 14 July 2014).

Wolverhampton's Learning2Go: https://www.wolverhampton-engage.net/sites/anonymous/Learning2GoOld/Pages/Whatis.aspx (accessed 22 July 2014).

Woodlawn School: http://www.woodlawn.org.uk/ (accessed 14 July 2014).

YouTube statistics: https://www.youtube.com/yt/press/en-GB/statistics.html (accessed 29 July 2014).

Znet.com. Malaysia Adopts Google Apps, Chromebooks for Education. www.zdnet.com/my/malaysia-adopts-google-apps-chromebooks-for-education-7000013847/ (accessed 14 July 2014).

Index

32; special educational needs 42; video snapshots 116; Woodlawn School 73, 74, 75
virtual learning environments (VLEs) 71, 123
visual impairments 39, 81
vocabulary 60, 69

Wales 7
websites 14, 15, 20, 55
Westfield Primary 92–3
Whatsapp 125
Which? 15, 20, 36n6
whole-school approach 67
Whyley, David 5, 10, 111, 116, 117, 119, 121n6
Wick High School 89, 90–1, 92, 96
Wikipedia 47

wikis 113
Wild Knowledge 4
Windows 9, 21; Essa Academy 65; Normanby Primary School 52; Windows 8 13, 17, 26–7, 31; Windows RT 26, 27
wireless network access 16–17, 61
Wishart, Jocelyn 115, 116
Woodlawn School 73–7
word processing 84
WordCoach 59
writing 58, 69, 114

Xbox Kinect 74
XP School 9

YouTube 21, 31, 32, 80, 125